Alexander Burak

What it Takes to be a Translator: Theory and Practice

Alexander Burak

What it Takes to be a Translator: Theory and Practice

LAP LAMBERT Academic Publishing

Impressum / Imprint

Bibliografische Information der Deutschen Nationalbibliothek: Die Deutsche Nationalbibliothek verzeichnet diese Publikation in der Deutschen Nationalbibliografie; detaillierte bibliografische Daten sind im Internet über http://dnb.d-nb.de abrufbar.

Alle in diesem Buch genannten Marken und Produktnamen unterliegen warenzeichen-, marken- oder patentrechtlichem Schutz bzw. sind Warenzeichen oder eingetragene Warenzeichen der jeweiligen Inhaber. Die Wiedergabe von Marken, Produktnamen, Gebrauchsnamen, Handelsnamen, Warenbezeichnungen u.s.w. in diesem Werk berechtigt auch ohne besondere Kennzeichnung nicht zu der Annahme, dass solche Namen im Sinne der Warenzeichen- und Markenschutzgesetzgebung als frei zu betrachten wären und daher von jedermann benutzt werden dürften.

Bibliographic information published by the Deutsche Nationalbibliothek: The Deutsche Nationalbibliothek lists this publication in the Deutsche Nationalbibliografie; detailed bibliographic data are available in the Internet at http://dnb.d-nb.de.

Any brand names and product names mentioned in this book are subject to trademark, brand or patent protection and are trademarks or registered trademarks of their respective holders. The use of brand names, product names, common names, trade names, product descriptions etc. even without a particular marking in this works is in no way to be construed to mean that such names may be regarded as unrestricted in respect of trademark and brand protection legislation and could thus be used by anyone.

Coverbild / Cover image: www.ingimage.com

Verlag / Publisher:
LAP LAMBERT Academic Publishing
ist ein Imprint der / is a trademark of
OmniScriptum GmbH & Co. KG
Heinrich-Böcking-Str. 6-8, 66121 Saarbrücken, Deutschland / Germany
Email: info@lap-publishing.com

Herstellung: siehe letzte Seite /
Printed at: see last page
ISBN: 978-3-659-51985-7

1

Table of Contents

To Galya – my Muse and dear wife.

Introduction

An important way that people interact with each other is translation. In fact, we are surrounded by translations without being consciously aware of it. High school and college lists of required readings, TV commercials, news on television and on the Internet, and many other transfers of information rely, to a very significant extent, on translation. The conventional understanding of translation embraces its interlingual variety, leaving aside its intralingual and intersemiotic varieties.[1] In this book I deal with interlingual translation: Russian-to-English and English-to-Russian. I define interlingual translation as the process and result of transferring complex clusters of meaning from one culture to another, using the language of the receiving culture to re-express those clusters of meaning as closely to the original as possible.

Today a lot of hope is being pinned on automated (computer) translation, based on computational ascending, descending, and combined descending-ascending algorithms. The latest trend – introduced on a wide scale by Google – relies on the "statistical" (probability of use) method of automated translation that uses large corpora of human-translated texts. The Google translation system (currently offering translations between 64 languages, which works out to 4,032 translation services) selects the most frequently occurring variants of translation in the vast data bank of translated texts that Google has accumulated. (It is not insignificant that all of these "raw material" texts have been initially translated by professional human translators.) In technical and legal translation, where subtlety of expression is normally replaced by clichés, this works pretty well, although the results usually need copy-editing by a "technical" translator – somebody specializing in the given subject field. It is hoped that an improved similar system will work well in translating much of popular, bestseller fiction – that variety of it which is mostly plot-driven, limited in the choice and originality of its vocabulary and style, and not known for much authorial "artistic" use of language. It is conceivable that machine-translated texts of such fiction prose might work as raw material to be further edited by a live translator. So it is not unreasonable to agree with some translation theorists and practitioners, like David Bellos, for example, that, for some practical, not too demanding purposes, automated translation – a kind of "Babel fish" solution – is possible. The "Babel fish" was a fictional species of fish in Douglas Adams's series of science fiction

---

[1] For details of Roman Jakobson's classic division of translation into three general varieties, see his "On Linguistic Aspects of Translation" (1971: 260-6) and "Linguistics and Poetics" (1987: 62-94).

novels *The Hitchhiker's Guide to the Galaxy* (1979-1992). It was used as a biological universal translator. When the small, yellow, leechlike fish was inserted into the ear canal, it allowed the wearer to instantly understand anything said in any form of language and thus communicate with extraterrestrials and speakers of all the languages in the world.

Bellos is rather less optimistic, however, about the possibility of a "final," definitive solution to literary translation problems through computer translators like Google Translate,[2] although he is cautiously optimistic about the technology of speech recognition that would allow a widely available word processor to generate texts from "simple" everyday speech. He refers to some current research in some unspecified "New Jersey labs" that could well lead to creating a commercially viable, fully automated, high quality speech translation system (he abbreviates it as FAHQST): "I may not live to see or hear it, but many of you probably will: automated interpreting for the secondary orality of *predictable* international diplomatic prose, for tourist inquiries at hotel reception desks, and maybe for other uses as well [my italics]. You will soon enter the era of tertiary orality. It will be another world" (Bellos 2011: 272).

In my own personal experience, when it comes to translating highly imaginative, original narrative fiction, untrammeled live human speech, or even relatively straightforward editorial film scripts – automated translation is more of a hindrance than an effective tool; it practically guarantees serious damage to the aesthetics of a complex verbal work of art. Even the most expert human translators of complex narrative prose (see, for example, the subtle analyses of some translations from English into Italian in Tim Parks's excellent book *Translating Style: A Literary Approach to Translation – A Translation Approach to Literature* [2011]) are incapable of doing full justice to original literary texts, in which "an awful lot of things can be happening at once, perhaps contradicting each other, perhaps qualifying each other; as a result the translator may find that it is not possible to express all of these complications simultaneously in his or her language" (Parks 2011: 14).

With regard to the prospects of high-quality literary translation by machines, I side firmly with the famous Russian translator, lexicographer and translation theorist, professor Dmitrii Ivanovich Ermolovich (b. 1952). Ermolovich bases his conclusions on the ideas of the famous British mathematician Roger Penrose, who argues, in part, that even in the realm of mathematics not all problems or proofs can be resolved with

---

[2] The reader can try it out at http://translate.google.com/#.

the help of computational methods (Penrose 1996).[3] Ermolovich applies Penrose's conception to translation and concludes that in translating imaginative texts, reliance on computational algorithms is seriously deficient because the fluid complexity of a communicative situation cannot be resolved by computation alone. What is crucial for a given communicatively unique situation is a participant understanding not only of segmented semantic meanings of words, phrases and sentences deployed in such a situation (even if a description of a similar situation already exists) but also of the overall significance of these phrases and sentences in their *gestalt*-like interactions.

Automated translation is no less difficult to apply effectively to film, where the vicarious participation of the interpreter/translator in the visual-audio flow of the narrative is a must. In his article "The Blind Babel Fish" (which is also a reference to the Douglas Adams' novels), Ermolovich sets out convincing practical proof of this thesis using the original text and the Russian translation of the American popular television series "Desperate Housewives" (Ermolovich 2011).

Of course, in a world of simplification and universalization of cross-cultural interactions (not to say, their perceived mediocratization, which is sometimes speciously equated with an unquestioned wholesomeness of the processes of globalization), there arises the question: To what extent will that part of verbal communication that falls outside the realm of possible solutions via use of computational technology continue to be relevant to individuals? My answer is that – like with any kind of genuine art that relies on its creator's superior artistic skills and its beholder's level of and individual need for discernment and aesthetic satisfaction – subtle translations of sophisticated narrative fiction will continue to be in demand among a restricted section of the population still interested in and shaped by complex renderings of human subjectivity. As for the "Babel fish" from the Adams novels, as Ermolovich puts it, "even if it existed, it would translate exceptionally badly, especially in conditions of rapidly changing situations: located in the ear, the fish wouldn't be able to see anything and, having to operate exclusively from hearing, it would spew absolute translation garbage" (2011, 2/30: 71).

---

[3] Following Ermolovich, I refer here to Penrose's famous book *Shadows of the Mind: A Search for the Missing Science of Consciousness*. The book argues that human consciousness is not necessarily intelligible in terms of computational models. The brain's conscious activity essentially transcends the forms or possibilities of computation. Penrose illustrates his thesis via mathematical logic, including detailed discussions of Godel's proposition of incompleteness, Turing's machines and computabilities, quantum mechanics, and microbiology. He concludes that artificial intelligence and computer-controlled expert systems are capable of assisting local human expertise but will not be able to replace such expertise.

The complexity of particular instances of translating prose fiction cannot be grasped without a clear picture of the different aspects of translation as a cross-cultural activity. Part of the problem of the existing misconceptions concerning different kinds of translation and interpreting is the fact that the terminological apparatus of translation studies is still in the process of being developed. The overarching aim of this book is to clarify some important aspects of translation theory and practice in order to make translating and evaluating translations more transparent and more widely understood. In part I of the book (chapters 1-6), I give a brief overview of some topical issues of translation theory through the eyes of some leading theorists and practitioners of translation. In Part II (chapters 7-11), I consider the challenges involved in attaining the level of what I call "expert professionalism" in literary translation. I discuss some of the latest translation expertise studies that may have a soberingly disconcerting effect on those who consider themselves professional translators. Chapter 11 is devoted almost exclusively to the opinions of Russian translators on the state of translation in Russia.

Although the book is devoted almost exclusively to "written" literary translation (translation of literary prose), I intentionally exclude the term "literary translation" from the title of the book because the issues I consider are – to a significant extent – relevant to other kinds of translation, including interpretation ("oral" translation). I expect the book to be interesting and useful not only for students of Russian-to-English and English-to-Russian translation but also for beginning and practicing translators irrespective of their working languages.

Part I. Some Theoretical Considerations

In theory, theory and practice are the same, but in practice, they are not.

(Anonymous)

Life is translation, and we are all lost in it.

(James Merrill, quoted in May 1994: 141)

In his essay on books and writing, the 19th-century German philosopher Arthur Schopenhauer had this to say about clarity of expression:

> Obscurity and vagueness of expression is always and everywhere a very bad sign: for in ninety-nine cases out of a hundred it derives from vagueness of thought, which in turn comes from an original incongruity and inconsistency in the thought itself, and thus from its falsity. [...] Those who put together difficult, obscure, involved, ambiguous discourses do not really know what they want to say: they have no more than a vague consciousness of it which is only struggling towards a thought: often, however, they also want to conceal from themselves and others that they actually have nothing to say (Schopenhauer 1970: 204-205).

I always keep the philosopher's admonition in mind but, of course, not everything famous philosophers say is necessarily right. In the case of the humanities, "struggling towards a thought" is sometimes the all-important stepping stone, the proverbial thin edge of the wedge that may open the way to a useful insight and, maybe, a clearer expression, and perhaps even a crystal-clear thought. It is mostly some of such bleeding-edge "strugglings towards a thought" that I will consider in part I of my book.

Chapter 1

Walter Benjamin: Aesthetics vs. Literalism?

Walter Benjamin (1892-1940) was a German philosopher, sociologist, literary and cultural critic, translator and essayist. In his extraordinarily frequently quoted essay "The Task of the Translator" (1923) Benjamin suggests that translation is a means to aspire to some divine "pure language" ("*die reine Sprache*"). "Pure language" is said to reside in the "suprahistorical kinship of languages" (Benjamin 1968: 74) that "rests in the intention underlying each language as a whole – an intention, however, which no single language can attain by itself but which is realized only by the totality of their intentions supplementing each other: pure language" (Benjamin 1968: 74). [...] "Translation thus ultimately serves the purpose of expressing the central reciprocal relationship between languages. It cannot possibly reveal or establish this hidden relationship itself; but it can represent it by realizing it in embryonic or intensive form" (72). Now if this means anything, it is that translation is a fiendishly difficult business and that the translator's goal – pure language – is something unattainable. Anyone who seeks a clear answer to the question of what exactly the translator's task is will likely be confused and disappointed. He or she may well conclude that Benjamin is a proponent of utranslatability. But this is not so. According to Benjamin, translation is possible if it is maximally literal. At the same time, meaning is secondary as "...no case for literalness can be based on a desire to retain the meaning." Instead, we are supposed to translate the multiple intentionality of the totality of existing languages. "[...] the significance of fidelity as ensured by literalness is that the work reflects the great longing for linguistic complementation. A real translation is transparent; it does not cover the original, does not block its light, but allows the pure language, as though reinforced by its own medium, to shine upon the original all the more fully" (79). "Therefore, it is not the highest praise of a translation, particularly in the age of its origin (sic!?), to say that it reads as if it had originally been written in that language" (79).

To keep things in perspective, one has to remember that when he wrote his "The Task of the Translator," Benjamin was a thirty-year-old man, and the piece itself was his introduction to his translation of Baudelaire's *Tableaux Parisiens* (Baudelaire 1923). It was not meant to be a scholarly disquisition on translation. It was only after he became famous, owing to his other writings, that everything Benjamin wrote, including "The Task of the Translator," began to be treated as gospel truth and became part of the canon of comparative literary studies and postmodernist thinking in general. I find Benjamin's definitions of "pure language" and the task of the translator vague and contradictory. Things become even more confused and confusing when Benjamin posits the question: "Is a translation meant for readers who do not understand the original?" The response he gives is disconcerting and discouraging (I know that some people won't agree with me): "In the appreciation of a work of art or an art form, consideration of the receiver never proves fruitful… Art […] posits man's physical and spiritual existence, but in none of its works is it concerned with his response. No poem is intended for the reader, no picture for the beholder, no symphony for the listener" (Benjamin 1968: 69). It follows that the receiver of the translation is, for all intents and purposes, taken out of the picture.

Among the countless reverential comments on Benjamin's contribution to translation studies, an interesting, somewhat discordant interpretation of Benjamin's essay is provided by Sarah Dudek, a philosophy and literature scholar from Germany. In her essay "Walter Benjamin and the Religion of Translation," Dudek, who is a native German speaker, suggests that the German title of the essay "*Die Aufgabe des Übersetzers*" might also mean "The Surrender of the Translator."[4] One of the central questions in Dudek's essay is "How can a theory that is so enigmatic, mystical and restrictive at the same time exert such an influence on the theory of translation? As is known, an extraordinary amount of theorizing referring to Benjamin's theory of translation has been produced by renowned authors such as Peter Szondi, Paul de Man, Jacques Derrida and scores of others?"[5] Dudek's answer is that Benjamin's theory makes sense if one focuses only on aesthetics: "If the world is understood as language then it follows that aesthetics is the only thing that makes sense. To go with the early Nietzsche one can state that the world is only justified if considered an aesthetic phenomenon."[6] That is all well and good, but – together with Leonard Koren, for example – I have to ask, "Which 'aesthetics' do you mean?" – the question used as the title of Koren's 2010 book, subtitled "Ten Definitions" (Koren 2010). Furthermore, focusing on "aesthetics" does not exactly address the

---

[4] Dudek: http://www.cipherjournal.com/html/dudek_benjamin.html. There may well be – and I suspect there are – other little subtleties and connotations that may not have come through in Harry Zohn translation – most likely, through no fault of his own – but his is the one translation that is universally available and accepted in the English-speaking world.

[5] Ibid.

[6] Ibid.

task of the translator. For all intents and purposes, Banjamin outlines a very general and vague outlook on the role of language in life: the world is language and what matters in it is aesthetics, whatever that may be. Aesthetics or no aesthetics, I think Dudek is right in concluding that Benjamin's position with regard to translation is more of a religion than a translation theory.

At the beginning of his essay, Benjamin's asks the question, "[…] do we not generally regard as the essential substance of a literary work what it contains in addition to information – as even a poor translator will admit – the unfathomable, the mysterious, the 'poetic,' something that a translator can reproduce only if he is also a poet?" (Benjamin 1968: 69-70). In the context of the whole essay, the question contains a contradiction. Whereas elsewhere in the essay Benjamin says that the translator cannot do full justice to the original, he now seems to be saying that it is possible for the translator to convey "the poetic" in the text, if he is also a poet. But I accept the question in terms of the Schopenhauerean "struggling toward a thought" and answer it with an emphatic "Yes." We *should* indeed regard as the essential substance of a literary work that which it contains in addition to straight information – something that Benjamin refers to as "the unfathomable and the mysterious." I wish, though, that Benjamin had provided a more concrete explication of "the unfathomable," "the mysterious" and "the poetic" in his religion of translation.

In Dudek's words, the essay's "magic is evoked by its ambiguity and its holistic aesthetics. Although it is not a theory of untranslatability, it is hard to think of its practical influence on translators. […] the presupposition of his theory of translation is his 'messianic' theory of language. It is hard to think of seriously accompanying Benjamin in looking to language for such a messiah."[7] I agree that there is something magic about the essay, if only because it has cast such a long shadow in academe.

Benjamin's thesis that a deliberately literal translation would be an approximation to his extremely abstractly defined "pure language" is incapable of being empirically verified or falsified, which makes it irrelevant for the practicing translator. One has to agree with Benjamin, though, that the translator creates a new cultural entity consisting of the original text plus its translation(s) and ensuring the original's afterlife, or, one might say, "reincarnation." Clusters of such new cultural entities are a fundamental part of translation discourse and can and should form a

---

[7] Op. cit.

database for comparative translation studies, translation criticism, or translation variance studies as a new subfield of translation studies.

Throughout his essay, Benjamin is casting about for a definition of *"die reine Sparche"* (pure language) and the "task of the translator" only to end up with the elusive generalities and abstractions which sound more like an unacknowledged "surrender." In making an overall assessment of Benjamin's contribution to translation studies, I am driven to conclude that his thinking on the tasks of the translator is contradictory, vague, and charmingly naive. Its contribution to translation studies is only interesting from the perspective of pure philosophy and aesthetics of translation (strange though Benjamin's idea of aesthetics as literalness may be).

As for literalist translation as a translation strategy (lately known as "foreignization"), it cannot and should not be rejected out of hand. It had its uses in the past and it has its uses in the present. It is a legitimate translation strategy that is useful in some specific cases. For example, at one stage in his career, the famous Russian literary critic and translator Mikhail Gasparov was a confirmed adherent of literalist translation. He later reconsidered his position and advocated different variants of translation of the same original for different audiences. At the peak of the flourishing of the "Soviet school of translation" in the 1960s and 70s, interlinear, word-for-word translations (*"podstrochniki"*) of poetry from numerous local languages of the Soviet Union into Russian were commonly used as "raw material" for Soviet poets to turn into verses. It was standard operating procedure. Today literalist translation is the foundation of the celebrity status of the translators Richard Pevear and Larissa Volokhonsky. Larissa Volokhonsky first creates very literalist interlinear translations of Russian literary texts for her husband Richard to polish up in English, after which they jointly edit and turn out the final text. For all intents and purposes, Pevear and Volokhonsky are faithful present-day keepers of Benjamin's legacy. And literalism (a. k. a. "foreignization") is far from dead.

Chapter 2

Jacque Derrida and John Searle: Deconstructing and Debunking

Jacques Derrida (1930-2004) was a French philosopher who is known as the founder of the concept and theory of deconstruction. A supplemental concept and theory of différance is also widely known. His prodigious amount of writings has had a significant influence on literary theory, philosophy, and translation studies. The number of references to Derrida by writers on translation studies automatically makes him a mandatory and interesting topic for discussion in this book. The difficulty with Derrida is that his verbose formulations are filled with vague, content-shifting terminology ever in the process of development. According to Mitchell Stephens,[8] writing on January 23, 1994 in *The New York Times Magazine*, Derrida had tried to explain his concept of "deconstruction" "many times, in many ways, not always with success."[9] For example, speaking at the Benjamin N. Cardozo School of Law, in New York in 1993, Derrida had this to say about deconstruction: "Needless to say, one more time, deconstruction, if there is such a thing, takes place as the experience of the impossible."[10] Faced with the murkiness of Derrida's definitions, Stephens is forced to provide his own understanding – as per Derrida – of the concept of deconstruction, which goes as follows: "To deconstruct a 'text' (a term defined broadly enough to include the Declaration of Independence and a Van Gogh painting) means to pick it apart, in search of ways in which it fails to make the points it seems to be trying to make. Why would someone want to 'read' (defined equally broadly) like that? In order to experience the impossibility of anyone writing or saying (or painting) something that is perfectly clear, the impossibility of constructing a theory or method of inquiry that will answer all questions or the impossibility of fully comprehending weighty matters, like death. Deconstruction, in other words, guards against the belief – a belief that has led to much violence – that the world is simple and can be known with certainty. It confronts us with the limits of what it is possible for human thought to accomplish" (Stephens 1994). Stephens's is

---

[8] Mitchell Stephens was then Chairman of the Journalism and Mass-Communication Department at New York University.

[9] "Jacque Derrida and Deconstruction":
http://www.nyu.edu/classes/stephens/Jacques%20Derrida%20-%20NYT%20-%20page.htm

[10] Ibid., see also Derrida's obituary by Jonathan Kandell, entitled "Jacques Derrida, Abstruse Theorist, Dies at 74", in *The New York Times* of October 10, 2004:
http://www.nytimes.com/2004/10/10/obituaries/10derrida.html

the clearest interpretation of Derrida's concept of "deconstruction" and of his general philosophy that I have ever happened to come across. I have to admit, though, that, for the most part, I seem to understand Derrida only by reading interpretations of his interpretations of himself by other interpreters.

The peculiar "otherness" of Derrida's writings in French is reflected in their barely penetrable English translations. As mentioned earlier, quite commonly, Derrida's interpretation of an interpretation had to be interpreted once again – in some cases by the translator – to make the reader's expectedly tenuous grasp of what Derrida is talking about a little less shaky. As a case in point, here is an excerpt from Peggy Kamuf's translator's note introducing her translation from the French of *The Ear of the Other* [*L'oreille de l'autre*], originally published in Montreal in 1982:

> English readers encountering Derrida's writing for the first time may be disconcerted by the dense mixing of styles, the demanding syntax, and a lexicon that expands the limits of the most unabridged dictionary. Of these lexical supplements, the term *différance* – which occurs several times in the following pages – requires special mention, although the full implication of its use within Derrida's thought cannot be summarized here. (The reader is referred to the essay "Différance" in *Margins of Philosophy* [1982].) Derrida forges this word at the intersection of the spatial and temporal senses of the verb *différer*: to differ and to defer. The standard spelling of the noun *différence* corresponds only to the first, spatial sense; there is no standard noun formed from the second sense of temporal deferral. The *-ance* ending conforms to the orthographics of a middle voice: neither active, nor passive, both active and passive (as in reson*ance*). With the term, Derrida designates the movement of differentiation and deferral, spacing and temporalization which must be thought of as preceding and comprehending any positioning of identifiable differences and oppositions. Significantly for Derrida's deconstruction of the traditional, philosophical opposition of speech and writing, the difference between *différence* and *différance* is unpronounced" (Derrida 1985a: xi-xii).

I became especially interested in *The Ear of the Other* because one of the blurbs on the back cover of the book says: "No writer has probed the riddle of *the Other* [my italics] with more patience and insight than Jacques Derrida... By rigorously interrogating the writings of major Western figures, Derrida not only forces a rethinking of the nature of reading and writing but calls into question basic assumptions about ourselves and our world..." – *Mark C. Taylor, Los Angeles Times*

Book Review (Derrida 1985a). (The reversed mirror reflection of the letter "a" in the title of the book suggests the impossibility of hearing – in the wide sense of the word – the Other in its/his/her/their entirety.)[11] But, more importantly, my interest was aroused by "Section III: Roundtable on Translation" of *The Ear of the Other*, which I expected to contain some interesting thoughts on translation. But I was in for a disappointment as, in this section of the book, Derrida is mostly echoing (sometimes nearly verbatim) Benjamin's "The Task of the Translator." The beginning part of Derrida's lengthy contribution to the discussion (transcribed in the book) deals with how the translator ought to understand texts and what the translator's general task is:

> To understand a text as an original is to understand it independently of its living conditions – the conditions, obviously, of its author's life – and to understand it instead in its surviving structure [...]. Given the surviving structure of an original text – always a sacred text in its own way insofar as it is a pure original – the task of the translator is precisely to respond to this demand for survival which is the very structure of the original text [...]. [...] the translator must neither reproduce, represent, nor copy the original, nor even, essentially, care about communicating the meaning of the original. Translation has nothing to do with reception or communication or information" [...] (Derrida 1985a: 122).

Now, I find it hard to imagine or understand how any translator can divorce the vaguely outlined "surviving structure of the original text" from communicating its meaning, let alone "[having] nothing to do with reception or communication or information." It is also difficult to imagine how the translator can square the above translation philosophy with what Derrida goes on to say in the same breath – and the lengthy quote here is, unfortunately, unavoidable:

> Translation augments and modifies the original, which, insofar as it is living on, never ceases to be transformed and to grow. It modifies the original even as it also modifies the translating language. This process – transforming the original as well as the translation – is the translation contract between the original and the translating text. In this contract it is a question of neither representation nor reproduction nor communication; rather, the contract is destined to assure a survival, not only of a corpus or a text or an author but of languages [...]. A translation never succeeds in the pure and absolute sense of

---

[11] While reading the section, one has to make allowances for the peculiarities of oral speech (the section is a transcript of Derrida's oral answers to questions from the participants in a colloquium held at the University of Montreal in 1979).

the term. Rather, a translation succeeds in promising success, in promising reconciliation. There are translations that don't even manage to promise, but a good translation is one that enacts that performative called a promise with the result that through the translation one sees the coming shape of a possible reconciliation among languages. It is then that one has the sense or the presentiment of what language itself is – "*die reine Sprache.*" Pure language, says Benjamin, is not one that has been purified of anything; rather, it is what makes a language a language, what makes for the fact that there is language [...]. This is what we learn from a translation, rather than the meaning contained in the translated text, rather than this or that particular meaning. We learn that there is language, that language is of language, and that there is a plurality of languages which have that kinship with each other coming from their being languages. This is what Benjamin calls pure language, "*die reine Sprache,*" the being-language of language. The promise of a translation is that which announces to us this being-language of language: there is language, and because there is something like language, one is both able and unable to translate" (Derrida 1985a: 122-124).

Taken as whole, Derrida's statements are – to put it in the kindest possible terms – internally competitive, although two statements in the above quote – if taken separately and out of the whole context, make perfectly good sense, banal adages though they essentially may be. These are: "Translation augments and modifies the original [...] even as it also modifies the translating language" and "A translation never succeeds in the pure and absolute sense of the term." Nor – I would add from myself – does Derrida's philosophy of translation.

A longtime and consistent critic of Derrida's version of postmodernism or relativism or "perspectivalism" is the American philosopher John R. Searle (b. 1932).[12] Over the last 40 years or so Searle has been a staunch defender of the scientific method of inquiry launched by the Enlightenment's scientific and philosophical program. In an interview with *Reason Magazine* published in February 2000, when asked whether Jacques Derrida was making bad arguments, or was just

---

[12] At the time of this writing John R. Searle was the Slusser Professor of the Philosophy of Mind and Language at the University of California at Berkeley. He has written extensively on "big issues" such as the nature of reality, the mind-body problem, the nature of consciousness, language and speech acts, and others, thereby developing his own theory of rationality in contradistinction to variable rationalities that seem to be the corollary of postmodernist thinking (see, for example, Searle 2002: 312-325).

being misread, Searle had this to say about Derrida's philosophy and the mistaken association of Derrida with Michel Foucault:

> With Derrida, you can hardly misread him, because he's so obscure. Every time you say, "He says so and so," he always says, "You misunderstood me." But if you try to figure out the correct interpretation, then that's not so easy. I once said this to Michel Foucault, who was more hostile to Derrida than I am, and Foucault said that Derrida practiced the method of *obscurantisme terroriste* (terrorism of obscurantism). We were speaking French. And I said, "What the hell do you mean by that?" and he said, "He writes so obscurely you can't tell what he's saying, that's the obscurantism part, and then when you criticize him, he can always say, 'You didn't understand me; you're an idiot.' That's the terrorism part. And I like that. So I wrote an article about Derrida. I asked Michel if it was OK if I quoted that passage, and he said yes" (Postrel and Feser 2000: 2).

Searle is not just anti-Derrida, he is anti-postmodernism in general, not least because postmodernism, from the 1960s until quite recently, was so pervasive in the American academe (see also Searle 1983/84, 1993, 2009). Searle believes that the essence of postmodernism is its conception of "alternative epistemic systems," which are systems "used to acquire knowledge and justify claims to knowledge" (Searle 2009: 90). Searle equates their postmodernist variety with "truly dreadful arguments":

> It is much easier to refute a bad argument than to refute a truly dreadful argument. A bad argument has enough structure that you can point out its badness. But with a truly dreadful argument, you have to try to reconstruct it so that it is clear enough that you can state a refutation. [...] But what about the truly dreadful arguments in such authors as Jacques Derrida, Jean-François Lyotard, and other postmodernists that have been more influential during the last half-century? What about, for example, Derrida's attempts to "prove" that meanings are inherently unstable and indeterminate, and that it is impossible to have any clear determinate representation of reality? (He argues, for example, that there is no tenable distinction between writing and speech.) (Searle 2009: 89-90.)

For Searle, postmodernism with its "alternative epistemic systems," is a mode of thinking with the help of which "we justify our beliefs using one epistemic system but somebody might have a different epistemic system that would give different results from ours" (Searle 2009: 90). Searle strongly opposes this mode of thinking and says that "the hypothesis of alternative epistemic rationalities has no clear meaning" (see Searle 2009: 91). When asked by a student, "What is your argument for rationality?" Searle responded, "That is an absurd question. There cannot be an argument for rationality because the whole notion of an argument presupposes rationality" (Searle 2009: 91). Searle's position is that of "metaphysical realism" – a rigorous defense of reason, objectivity, and intellectual honesty and courage within the academy.

If Derrida's writings are too abstract, inconsistent, and not providing direct answers to translation problems, despite making considerable claim to doing so, Searle's criticism of Derrida's life and language philosophy is overly categorical, although very consistent and logical. Searle's problem is that he underestimates the value of little insights spread over the voluminous, contradictory, discursive writings by thinkers such as Lacan, Bourdieu, Lyotard, and Derrida, to name just a few – especially if and when they become widely read and commented upon in academe. From my perspective, these thinkers make insightful claims and create new concepts, "content-shifting" though these may be. Such concepts may be filled with new content and may conceivably be applied in ways and in fields of study and research those thinkers themselves did not envision. Despite frequent references to Derrida in the translation studies literature, he has not advanced any clear-cut translation theory besides commenting obliquely on translation from the perspective of his key concepts of "deconstruction" and "différance" and referring continually to Benjamin's legendary "The Task of the Translator." Proceeding from the way I understand Derrida's two key concepts "deconstruction" and "différance, I can define the task of the translator as negotiating the physical (textual) and temporal (separated by a period of time) differences (the "différance") between original and translation, contingently determined by the translator's professional expertise deployed in specific sociocultural contexts. In the world according to Derrida, such differences have an ineffable nature. In the world according to Searle, they are embraceable by common sense and capable of being verbalized in concrete terms. In a mutually complementary sense, both thinkers are right: we have to accept the inevitability of potential multiplicity of translations of the same imaginative piece of writing (this follows from Derrida's ideas), but each of those inevitably different translations can only be arrived at through a process of concrete, rationally perceived translation strategies and operations – something that follows from Searle's thinking. Translation is impossibly difficult but unavoidable, being the primary constitutive medium of cross-cultural interactions.

Chapter 3

George Steiner: "Hermeneutic Motion"

One of the most significant and oft-quoted books in the field of translation studies in recent decades has been *After Babel: Aspects of Language and Translation* (1975/92/98) by George Steiner (b. 1929), an influential European-born, British-American literary critic, philosopher, translator, essayist, and educator. Steiner – while referring to Ortega y Gasset's *Miseria y esplebdor de la traducción* [The Misery and Splendor of Translation] – agrees with the Spanish philosopher and writer that "translation *is* impossible [...] but so is absolute concordance between thought and speech" (Steiner 1998: 264), and concludes that "somehow the 'impossible' is overcome at every moment in human affairs" (Steiner 1998: 264).

Steiner comes out strongly in support of essential translatability of any text by stating his opposition to what he calls the "monadist" position in translation. The term "monadist" is derived from "monad" (from the Greek "monas" – unit or "monos" – alone), which was a central concept in the later metaphysics of the German philosopher Gottfried Wilhelm von Leibnitz (1646-1716). A "monad" is "a simple indestructible non-spatial element regarded as the unit of which reality consists of."[13] Steiner gives the following historical reference regarding his usage of "nomadist":

> In 1697, in his tract on the amelioration and correction of German, Leibnitz put forward the all-important suggestion that language is not the vehicle of thought but its determining medium. Thought is language internalized, and we think and feel as our particular language impels and allows us to do. But tongues differ as profoundly as do nations. They too are monads, "perpetual living mirrors of the universe," each of which reflects or, as we would now put it, structures experience according to its own particular sight-lines and habits of cognition (Steiner 1998: 78).

Steiner understands a "monadist" perspective on language to hold "that universal deep structures are either fathomless to logical and psychological investigation or of an order so abstract, so generalized as to be well-nigh trivial. [...] The extreme 'monadist' position – we shall find great poets holding it – leads logically to the belief that real translation is impossible. What passes for translation is a convention

---

[13] http://encyclopedia2.thefreedictionary.com/monad

of approximate analogies, a rough-cast similitude, just tolerable when the two relevant languages or cultures are cognate, but altogether spurious when remote tongues and far-removed sensibilities are in question" (Steiner: 77; see also Leighton: 181).

Steiner vigorously opposes the "monadist approach" stating that this "argument from perfection […] is facile. No human product can be perfect. No duplication, even of materials which are conventionally labeled as identical, will turn out a total facsimile. Minute differences and asymmetries persist. To dismiss the validity of translation because it is not always possible and never perfect is absurd. What does need clarification, say the translators, is the degree of fidelity to be pursued in each case, the tolerance allowed as between different jobs at work" (264). "In brief: translation is desirable and possible. Its methods and criteria need to be investigated in relation to substantive, mainly 'difficult' texts" (266).

In contradistinction to "monadic" or "perfectionist" views on translation, Steiner formulates his own "hermeneutic" perspective on the process of translation. According to Steiner, translation consists of a series of stages that interconnect and form the "hermeneutic motion" of the translator's thinking in the course of producing a translation. This "hermeneutic motion," or "the act of elicitation and appropriative transfer of meaning, is fourfold" (1998: 312). First, "there is initiative trust, an investment of belief […] in the 'other', as yet untried, unmapped alternity of statement" that "concentrates to a philosophically dramatic degree the human bias towards seeing the world as symbolic, as constituted of relations in which 'this' can stand for 'that', and must in fact be able to do so if there are to be meanings and structures" (1998: 312). "After trust comes aggression. The second move of the translator is incursive and extractive" (313). In explicating this stage in his hermeneutical theory of translation, Steiner develops Heidegger's idea that "understanding is not a matter of method but of primary being, that 'being consists in the understanding of other being' into [sic!] the more naïve, limited axiom that each act of comprehension must appropriate another entity (we translate *into*). […] The translator invades, extracts, and brings home" (313-314). This is the stage of the appropriation of "the other", the Derridean deconstruction stage, or the stage of interpretation of the original text that is, in large part, unique to a given translator. "The third movement is incorporative, in the strong sense of the word" (314). The clash of "the other" that is being imported with the domesticating or host culture is traumatic for both sides:

The import, of meaning and of form, the embodiment, is not made in or into a vacuum. The native semantic field is already extant and crowded. There are innumerable shadings of assimilation and placement of the newly-acquired, ranging from a complete domestication, an at-homeness […] all the way to the permanent strangeness and marginality of an artifact such as Nabokov's 'English-language' *Onegin*. But whatever the degree of 'naturalization', the act of importation can potentially dislocate or relocate the whole of the native structure" (314-315).

After the third stage, "the hermeneutic motion is dangerously incomplete" (316). The system of cross-cultural interaction is "off-tilt" (316). The fourth stage is "the enactment of reciprocity." It is necessary in order to restore balance between original and translation. Restoring this balance is "the crux of the *métier* and morals of translation. But it is very difficult to put abstractly" (316). And indeed it is – as the following statement by Steiner will confirm: "The appropriative 'rapture' of the translator – the word has in it, of course, the root and meaning of violent transport – leaves the original with a dialectically enigmatic residue" (316). This is the stage where, in my view, the translator leaves his or her own unique imprint on the translation. Later in the text, Steiner resorts to less elaborate language and describes this stage as "compensation" or "restitution":

The translation restores the equilibrium between itself and the original, between source-language and receptor-language which had been disrupted by the translator's interpretative attack and appropriation. The paradigm of translation stays incomplete until reciprocity has been achieved, until the original has regained as much as it had lost. '*Pour comprendre l'autre,*' wrote Massignon in his famous study of the 'internal syntax' of Semitic tongues, "*il ne faut pas se l'annexer, mais devenir son hôte.*"[14] […] Translation recompenses in that it can provide the original with a persistence and geographical-cultural range of survival which it would otherwise lack (415-416).

A conceptualization of culture is something of an afterthought in Steiner's perspective. He suggests a "topological" definition of culture, borrowing the mathematical concept of topology. "Topology is the branch of mathematics which deals with those relations between points and those fundamental properties of a figure which remain invariant when that figure is bent out of shape (when the rubber

---

[14] To understand the other, don't annex it – become its guest.

sheet on which we have traced the triangle is bent into conic or spherical shape)" (Steiner 1998: 448). "Defined 'topologically,' a culture is a sequence of translations and transformations of constants ('translation' always tends towards 'transformation')" (Steiner 1998: 449). Steiner is silent about how to extricate the cultural constants from those parts of a particular original and its translation(s) that are not constants. Unfortunately, together with concepts such as *"die reine Sprache,"* these constants are abstractions that seem to be beyond the translator's ontological and epistemological grasp.

In different parts of his book, Steiner talks about "a palimpsest of historical [and] political undertones and overtones" (180); "a 'chord' of associations" (180); "the irreducible singularity of personal remembrance" (182); "the 'association-net' of personal consciousness and subconsciousness" (182); "a semantic field" (314); "a dialectically enigmatic residue" (316); "formats of significance" (317); "the 'other' language and 'other' culture" (412); "the serious alternity of meaning and expressive form" (413); " a cultural lattice" (413), "the differing idiomatic habits, the distinct associative contexts which generate resistance and affinity between two different languages" (445). These concepts coalesce in Steiner's definition of the task of the translator, which, compared with Benjamin's and Derrida's, is much more clearly stated and realizable:

> The translator must actualize the implicit "sense", the denotative, connotative, illative,[15] intentional, associative range of significations which are implicit in the original, but which it leaves undeclared or only partly declared simply because the native auditor or reader has an immediate understanding of them (291).

Steiner's definition of translation is a classic of elegance:

> Good translation […] can be defined as that in which the dialectic of impenetrability and ingress, of intractable alienness and felt 'at-homeness' remains unresolved, but expressive. Out of the tension of resistance and affinity […] grows the elucidative strangeness of the great translation (Steiner 1998: 411).

Talking about the same original text that is often translated by several contemporary and subsequent translators, Steiner says that "such a sequence of alternative versions is an act of reciprocal, cumulative criticism and correction. […] the problems of mutual awareness and critique are exactly those posed by multiple

---

[15] Inferential: relating to or involving the drawing of inferences.

translation" (Steiner 1998: 438). In other words, multiplicity of translations of the same original is inevitable.

To conclude, Steiner's is an elegant theory, brilliantly expressed, even though, in places, it sounds somewhat tautological and seems to be torn between wishful thinking and self-fulfilling prophecies. His theory of translation as "hermeneutic motion" does not only suggest a useful general conceptual framework for translation studies but is also a treasure-trove of insights into numerous "accursed questions" of translation practice that many a student and practitioner of translation, myself included, is haunted by.

Chapter 4

Theories of the Middle Range: An "Operationalized" Approach to Translating and Assessing Translations

There is a constant tension between "grand" theory or general theory (highly abstract thinking about translation issues – like the ones outlined in the previous chapters) and practice (resolving concrete translation problems). From the perspective of high philosophy of translation, in order to be ontologically – or philosophically – correct and rigorous, one has to accept the universal principle of untranslatability[16] and abandon the whole idea of translating anything. On the other hand, from the perspective of translation practice, having a translation contract in hand "concentrates the mind wondrously," compelling one to circumvent this principle and deal with the practical realities of translation head-on and hands-on in real time. In Derrida's words, "translation is both necessary and impossible" (1985a: 103).

Given the serious tension between theory and practice, the question arises: "To what extent are grand narratives of translation theory relevant?" Grand narratives of translation (its general, highly abstract theories) are, of course, necessary, but their usefulness should not be overstated. Translation philosophy (an umbrella term that I use to designate the numerous general theories of translation) presents refined exercises for the mind and – as any philosophy – means "the love of wisdom," in our case, concerning translation. However, the highly abstract nature of general translation theory (or theories) trivializes it in the face of the very specific problems translators have to face on a daily basis.

Translation is a highly complex, cross-cultural, variance-prone activity, which is impossible to embrace with one neat theory. I advocate translation theories of the middle range. The concept of middle-range theories, as opposed to grand or general theories, was first developed by the American sociologist Robert Merton with reference to social thought (Merton: 1968). I apply his general conception to problems of translation. In my analyses I am also guided by Isaiah Berlin's idea that different aspects of beneficial phenomena or pursuits do not necessarily constitute a harmonious whole and may, in fact, come into conflict with one another (Berlin: 1997); in other words, pursuing one unquestionable good may well come into conflict with pursuing another, no less desirable good.

---

[16] See Chapters 1 and 2.

Robert K. Merton (1910-2003) was an outstanding American sociologist who is best known for developing several universally used concepts such as "unintended consequences," "role model," "self-fulfilling prophecy," "reference group," and others. He is less known for creating the concept "middle-range theory," which he developed to oppose the all-embracing word "theory." His problem with the word "theory" was that "like so many words which are bandied about, the word 'theory' threatens to become emptied of meaning. The very diversity of items to which the word is applied leads to the result that it often obscures rather than creates understanding" (Merton 1964: 5). In sociology, Merton advocated "theories of the middle range," which he defined as "theories intermediate to the minor working hypotheses evolved in abundance during the day-to-day routines of research, and the all-inclusive speculations comprising a master conceptual scheme from which it is hoped to derive a very large number of empirically observed uniformities..." (Merton 1964: 5-6).

What Merton said about social theory is, in my view, perfectly applicable to translation theory. As in the case of the search for a total system of sociological theory, trying to create a total translation theory, in which – to use Merton's words – "all manner of observations promptly find their preordained place," is a "premature and apocalyptic belief. We are not ready. The preparatory work has not yet been done" (Merton 1964: 6).

In the meantime, the American academe continues to be in the grip of its obsession with "theory," which, I think, is a survival of its obsession with postmodernism. To me, creating a translation theory that would explain everything by explaining nothing is obviously an exercise in futility. This is what postmodernism is particularly good at. Give me John Searle any day.

As I already mentioned, the reasonableness of a "middle-range approach" is also supported by Isaiah Berlin's relative values theory, according to which a single perceived good or positive value in and of itself (excellence, for example) does not necessarily form a harmonious, integral whole alongside other goods or values (like equality, for example) and its pursuit may, in fact be in conflict with the achievement of other, equally commendable goods or values (see Berlin 1997: 1-16).

Each of Steiner's four stages of a translation process (see chapter 3) that he illustrates with concrete examples is close to my idea of a middle-range theory. In my scheme of thinking, a middle-range translation theory starts with some readily perceivable and accessible empirical phenomena, such as word senses that can be found in dictionaries and that can be contrasted with their contextual use in translation; different types of sentence structure that are described in grammar books and that can be contrasted with their actual theme-rheme structures in translated texts; and the lexicological and stylistic parameters of text as described in relevant literature that can be contrasted with their actual implementation in different translations.

Translations of works of verbal art are a very special kind of cross-cultural discourse carried out between pairs of specific languages (in our case – Russian and American English) through the medium of a translator who tries to make sense of the sociocultural "other" through the prism of his or her subjectivity. The translator has to re-create the cross-cultural "other" in a context that is alien to and removed from the multifaceted local "other" in both time and space. This is a hugely complicated task that gets fulfilled with varying degrees of success, hence the variance in translations. In order to make translation discourse analysis practically significant, I operationalize its elements by examining the process of translation and its results from the perspectives of the semantics, syntax, and pragmatics of specific, existing texts.

At the level of the word, I single out nine concretely isolatable semantic parameters of word senses needed to be kept in mind while translating and analyzing the translation quality of other translations. These parameters are: sense core, sense periphery, type of emotion, intensity of emotion, evaluative judgment, style, dialect, frequency of occurrence, and pragmatic reference involving different aspects of the cultural setting of the translation. A notional word in a specific text is uniquely contextualized. All non-predicative, contextually bound phrases or word combinations (that is, phrases that do not contain the main verb(s) – the predicate(s) – of a sentence or clause) are also contextually unique (ad hoc) word senses possessed of the denotative and connotative components indicated above. Thus, for example, the non-predicative word combinations (phrases) "a latte-drinking, arugula-eating, wine-sipping, pacifistically-minded liberal" or "a knuckle-dragging, gun-toting, bible-thumping, Budweiser-swilling, America-the-best-minded conservative"[17] are basically two self-contained word senses possessing complex structures of denotative and connotative elements. The differences in the semantic composition of Russian and American lexical items and the ways these differences

---

[17] The two phrases can be translated, respectively, as "либерал-пацифист – любитель кофе-латте, рукколы и вина" and "помесь вооруженного дебила, религиозного фанатика, любителя пива 'Бадвайзер' и шовиниста-консерватора"

are negotiated in translation, are examined in detail in my book *Translating Culture-1: Words* (Moscow: R.Valent, 2010).

At the predication (sentence and clause) level, I distinguish a set of basic models or algorithms to reproduce different communicative structures of sentences and clauses in translating from Russian into English and vice versa. The central problem at the syntactic level of analysis is that the syntactic and semantic structures of sentences in Russian and in English often do not coincide. Syntax (the form of the sentence) and its communicative impact often collide. As a result the word order in the translation has to be brought into line with the communicative structure (the theme-rheme relationship) of the original sentence viewed in the wider context of the paragraph. A brief example illustrating just one transformational model where the predicate of the Russian sentence serves as a rheme and is placed at the end of the sentence will suffice to hint at the nature of the problem. Consider a simple sentence like the following: Какие-либо сомнения относительно благородства намерений руководителя американской делегации [subject – theme] у российских участников переговоров [explication of rheme] отсутствуют [rheme]. In English translation this will be recast in a very different form – possibly like this: The Russian participants in the negotiations [subject – theme] don't have any doubts [predicate – rheme] as to the noble motives of the leader of the American delegation [explication of rheme]. In my book *Translating Culture-2: Sentence and Paragraph Semantics* (Moscow: R.Valent, 2013), I identify a set of typical Russian sentence structures that are atypical of English and provide a detailed examination of ways of negotiating those syntactic discrepancies in translating theme-and-rheme patterns within the framework of paragraphs.

My most recent book, *"The Other" in Translation: A Case for Comparative Translation Studies* (Bloomington, Indiana: Slavica, 2013) focuses on the pragmatic aspects of "the other in translation," which include (1) the sociocultural identity of the creator of the original, (2) the cross-cultural correlation of the two texts' genres, (3) the cross-cultural correlation of the two texts' functional styles, (4) the sociocultural and historical circumstances in which the author created the original text, including the perceived significance of the text with reference to the other texts created in the same period, (5) the distinguishing features of the authorial style comprising the uniqueness of the lexis, syntax, prosody (the rhythmic flow of the text), and the cultural specificity of the narrative, (6) the cultural and linguistic "remainder" and *realia* that get or do not get translated, (7) the unique socio-cultural imprint or "residue" of the personality of the translator in the translated text, and (8) the sociocultural identity and the expectations of the receivers of the translation, whether the translator targets a specific audience or not.

I distinguish five clearly identifiable, if interpenetrating and overlapping, methods of or approaches to tackling "the other" in translating narrative fiction and films: neutralization, domestication, foreignization, contamination, and stylization. To a greater or lesser extent, all translators resort to these five strategies. In this latest book, I examine the above pragmatic issues, based on specific examples from prose fiction and voiceover film translations. It must be emphasized that in the face of the innumerable ramifications of translation discourse analysis, it is important to focus on a specific pair of languages and cultures as manifested in a concrete text or texts that can be conceivably analyzed and interpreted in great depth by a translation analyst, based on a specifically defined framework of criteria or textual parameters. Hence my consideration of all these translation aspects is confined to two specific languages – Russian and English. To reiterate, the focus of my analyses is the text viewed as a coherent and cohesive series of sentences constituting a communicatively complete situation and fulfilling certain socio-cultural informative and aesthetic functions. A tiny example of the different pragmatics of translation resorted to by different translators can be illustrated by the three different translations of the first sentence in J. D. Salinger's *The Catcher in the Rye*:

J.D. Salinger (1951) *The Catcher in the Rye*	Рита Райт-Ковалева (1960) *Над пропастью во ржи*
If you really want to hear about it, the first thing you'll probably want to know is where I was born, and what my lousy childhood was like, and how my parents were occupied and all before they had me, and all that David Copperfield kind of crap, but I don't feel like going into it, if you want to know the truth (Salinger 1991: 1).	Если вам на самом деле хочется услышать эту историю, вы, наверно, прежде всего захотите узнать, где я родился, как провел свое дурацкое детство, что делали мои родители до моего рождения, словом, всю эту дэвид-копперфилдовскую муть. Но, по правде говоря, мне неохота в этом копаться (2010а: 5).
Максим Немцов (2008) *Ловец на хлебном поле*	Яков Лотовский (2010) *Над пропастью во ржи*
Если по-честному охота слушать, для начала вам, наверно, подавай, где я родился и что за погань у меня творилась в детстве, чего предки делали и всяко-разно, пока не	Если вы и в самом деле непрочь услышать обо всем об этом, вам сперва, наверно, захочется узнать из каких я мест, как прошло мое сопливое детство, род занятий моих

заимели меня, да прочую Дэвид-Копперфилдову херню, только не в жилу мне про все это трындеть, сказать вам правду (Salindzher 2008: 9).	родителей и прочую муру в духе Давида Копперфильда. Но, честно говоря, неохота в этом ковыряться (2010b: 2).

Translating Culture 1, *Translating Culture 2*, and *"The Other" in Translation* concretize – or "operationalize" – specific aspects or elements of such general theoretical perspectives as the poetics of translation, polysystem theory, the ideology of translation, etc. They are a complex of middle-range theories that can be empirically verified by applying it in the course of resolving a similar translation problem in a different stretch of language.

While acknowledging the importance of "theory," I believe that a lot of the oft-quoted thinking on translation – like that of Benjamin or Derrida, for example – is deployed on such a high plane of abstraction that it becomes practically meaningless and irrelevant when attempts are made to apply it on the ground. That said, it is not that abstract philosophical thought struggling with "the loose baggy monster" of translation is wrong, the problem is that concepts such as *die reiner Sprache* (pure language) (Benjamin 1923/68: 74, 80), for example, – which cannot be proved or falsified using both the scientific method and any qualitative approaches – are not so much guides to translation as interesting mental exercises or mental distractions not necessarily conducive to practical solutions. As for qualitative methods of translation discourse analysis, I have to devote the next chapter to clearing their bad name given to them by stern adherents of empirical – "truly scientific" – methods of research and analysis.

Chapter 5

Qualitative Methods: A Case for Comparative Translation Studies

Quite undeservedly, qualitative methods of research and analysis have been given a bad reputation on the fallacious grounds that they are "not empirical enough," i. e. they do not employ enough "measurements" or "metrics." But this is an assumption that follows from a one-sided approach to research. I submit that the main reason for the widespread misconceptions about qualitative methods of research is that it is easier to set up an experiment in the natural sciences, which seek a syllogism-driven, single, replicable result, than to force the "crooked timber of humanity" – manifested, in our case, in the multiple possibilities of translating – into the Procrustean bed of the "hard" sciences. In the humanities, especially when analyzing the fluidity of sociolinguistic discourse (embedded in individual subjectivity), the rigid simplicity and materiality of hard metrics is often unrewarding and sometimes downright misleading. Of course, it feels much more comfortable to have definitive, hard answers than to accept the "unbearable lightness of being." There is also no escaping the fact that the answers in the humanities more often than not outline sociocultural tendencies – not hard and fast physical realities. But, in the final analysis, it is the multiple and elusive existential solutions that fill the proverbial pursuit of happiness with individually meaningful content and provide at least approximate orientations in defining one's purpose in life. The making and reading of translations is both a "scientific" and a humanistic pursuit. Translation is a science and an art rolled into one, in which qualitative principles of research play a very significant role.

Ideally, quantitative or empirical methods of research should be complemented with qualitative ones and vice versa. However, in sociological and other kinds of humanities research there are quite often situations when predominantly quantitative techniques cannot be applied because of the nature of the object of study. When the set of items or data from which a statistically representative sample would normally be drawn[18] is impossible to define and single out precisely, because it is too disparate and diffuse, the researcher resorts to case studies, focus groups and other instruments of research, involving a strong element of qualitative judgment. In our case, both the population of translators and the universe of the original texts and their translations are too disparate to determine precisely. Consequently, a statistically – or empirically

---

[18] In sociological research, such a set of items or individuals is called "population," or "universe."

– "valid" sample of texts is impossible to form. I therefore advocate "comparative translation discourse analysis" in the form of case studies[19] as a practically applicable and theoretically substantiated form of analysis in working out translation solutions and assessing existing translations. The kind of case studies I develop is firmly grounded in the empirical reality of the source and translation texts, whose parameters are very tangible.[20]

According to Keith Punch, an Australian research theorist, "a dominant feature of present day qualitative research is its diversity" (Punch 1998: 139). Given the diversity and complexity of the components of "the other" in a specific original text and its translation(s), we cannot and should not rely on one tidy idea to encompass everything, but certain principles do need to be established. For the most part, I adhere to the principles of qualitative research as defined by Denzin and Lincoln in their *Handbook of Qualitative Research* (1994) and Miles and Huberman in their *Qualitative Data Analysis* (1994). In view of the generally misunderstood and underrated status of the qualitative aspects of any kind of research, a somewhat extended summary of the recurrent elements in qualitative research is in order. I believe that the following principles are hard to dispense with in any kind of scholarly or scientific research, which in the final analysis is one and the same thing:

(1) Qualitative research is conducted through an intense and/or prolonged contact with a "field" of life situations. These situations are typically "banal" or normal ones, reflective of the everyday life of individuals, groups, societies, and organizations.

(2) The researcher's role is to gain a "holistic" overview of the context under study: its logic, its arrangements, and its explicit and implicit rules.

(3) The researcher attempts to capture data on the perceptions of local actors "from the inside," through a process of deep attentiveness, of empathetic understanding, and of suspending or "bracketing" preconceptions about the topics under discussion.

(4) [...] the researcher may isolate certain themes and expressions that can be reviewed with informants [...].

---

[19] See my book *"The Other" in Translation: A Case for Comparative Translation Studies* (Bloomington, Indiana: Slavica, 2013).

[20] The book *"The Other" in Translation: A Case for Comparative Translation Studies* is an illustration of my methodology.

(5) A main task is to explicate the ways people in particular settings come to understand, account for, take action, and otherwise manage their day-to-day situations.

(6) Many interpretations of [...] material are possible, but some are more compelling for theoretical reasons or on grounds of internal consistency.

(7) Relatively little standardized instrumentation is used at the outset. The researcher is essentially the main "measurement device" in the study.

(8) Most analysis is done with words. The words can be assembled, subclustered, broken into semiotic segments. They can be organized to permit the researcher to contrast, compare, analyze, and bestow patterns upon them ["] (Miles and Huberman as quoted in Punch 1998: 149).

In advocating and conducting comparative (or contrastive) translation discourse analysis (CTDA), I proceed from the empirically incontrovertible fact that translations, whether written or oral, exist in a physical form and may serve as the object or subject of concrete research and analysis. But CTDA goes beyond textual analysis. It also factors in the sociocultural specificity of translators. Translators are not just highly skilled language manipulators but also cultural mediators. Their work creates and adjusts the cultures in which they operate. This influence is exerted through translated texts, which are linguistically codified experiences. Thus the primary objects of CTDA are original texts and their translations, including the perceived unique linguocultural imprint of the specific translator/s on the text/s of the translation.

Comparative translation discourse analysis involves several interdependent operations: (1) establishing the perceived educational, sociocultural, entertainment, and aesthetic effects of the original text on its domestic audience; (2) identifying the linguistic means with the help of which those effects are achieved in the original text; (3) determining the degree of approximation of the effects of the selected translation/s on their supposed audiences as compared to the effects of the original text on its domestic audiences; and (4) identifying the linguistic means that the specific translator/s used to achieve the established degree of approximation of the effects of the translation/s on the supposed cross-cultural audience in comparison with the perceived effects of the original of the translation in its source culture. All of these operations result in providing to the translator or translation analyst with what I call a *tertium comparationis* of semantic, structural-communicative, and pragmatic criteria to be used as a template for comparing original and translation. Put differently, the *tertium comparationis* of the translation analyst is constituted by his or her comparative perceptions of original and translation. It can be tested on native speakers coming from respective cultures and other translators working with the same pair of languages. My aims in such analyses and interpretations are to trace the modus operandi of the translators and to evaluate their sociocultural impact.

The particulars of the contrastive method of studying cross-cultural translation discourse through prose fiction in Russian and in English can be concretized by asking and answering the following key questions:

(1) With reference to the sender: What is the socio-cultural identity of the original creator of a text (written or spoken)? What are the choice of words, general language style, and narrative preferences of the sender?

(2) With reference to the topic of the message: How do the original and its translation(s) compare as to the perceived basic denotational (dictionary, cognitive) meanings contained in the original message and its translation? How and to what extent – if at all – have the *realia* and "the Lecerclean remainder"[21] been incorporated into the translated text?

(3) With reference to the message form or message poetics, as defined above: What are the original authorial textual manipulations, if any, that are producing the perceived aesthetic effect on the receiver of the original and how can these manipulations be duplicated by the translator to achieve a conceivably similar effect on the receiver of the translation? What points of tension are there between the conventional functional styles of the two languages in general and the authorial style of the original and its replication, if any, in the translated text? How do the original and its translation(s) compare as to the perceived connotational meanings contained in the message?

(4) With reference to the code of the message (text): What are the linguistic, stylistic, dialectal, idiolectal, and terminological features that characterize the original text and how can they be duplicated for similar effect in the translated text?

(5) With reference to the receiver of the translation(s) (its or their audiences): Who are the intended socio-cultural contingents? What are, conceivably, their expectations with regard to the translated text? To what extent can and should those expectations be met?

Translations of works of verbal art are a very special kind of cross-cultural discourse carried out between pairs of specific languages (in our case – Russian and American English) through the medium of a translator who tries to make sense of the

---

[21] See *The Violence of Language* by Jean-Jacques Lecercle (Routledge, 1990).

sociocultural "other" through the prism of his or her subjectivity. The translator has to re-create the cross-cultural "other" in a context that is alien to and removed from the multifaceted local "other" in both time and space. This is a hugely complicated task that gets fulfilled with varying degrees of success, hence the variance in translations. In order to make translation discourse analysis practically significant, I operationalize its elements by examining the process of translation and its results from the perspectives of the semantics, syntax, and pragmatics of specific, existing texts (see chapter 4).

Based on the principles and strategies outlined so far, I will have the audacity to state that the explanatory power of the underestimated qualitative methods of research – and CTDA is my version of them – is not all that much lower than, say, the explanatory power of the standard model of modern physics (the queen of the sciences), which does not incorporate gravity, for example, or explain the invisible dark matter that makes up 80 percent of the universe. Generally speaking, as the British-born American theoretical physicist and mathematician Freeman Dyson puts it, "[…] science is only a small part of human capability. We gain knowledge of our place in the universe not only from science but also from history, art, and literature. Science is a creative interaction of observation with imagination. […] Imagination by itself can still enlarge our vision when observation fails. […] All of science is uncertain and subject to revision. The glory of science is to imagine more than we can prove. […] Hermann Weyl, who was one of the main architects of the relativity and quantum revolution, said […], 'I always try to combine the true with the beautiful, but when I have to choose one or the other, I usually choose the beautiful'" (Dyson 2012: 39).

Chapter 6

Pseudo and Real Translation Reviews

In asserting a middle-range comparative approach in translation studies outlined in chapters 4 and 5, I am countering a trend that manifests itself in spurious reviews of translated literary works. One would expect such reviews to include at least elements of comparative translation analyses, but they practically never do. To paraphrase Venuti,[22] I call the approach adopted in the majority of literary translation reviews misguided aestheticism. Such "aesthetic" reviews are usually elegantly-phrased, scholarly-sounding disquisitions on – supposedly – the quality of translations that have just been published or are about to be published. They are provided by prominent writing figures, who – more often than not – do not have a sufficient knowledge of the original texts whose translations they are discussing or have no such knowledge at all. This means that no genuine comparative analysis of original and translation is actually made. This is what I call misguided aestheticism or pseudo translation reviewing – or "belletrism," to use Venuti's term.[23]

The absence of serious comparative analyses of the artistic qualities of the original text written in one language and its representation as translation in another is harmful to the author/s of the translation because such an absence obfuscates the essential issues of translation and the fact that it is a high art requiring years of deliberate practice. (I will deal with the question of what deliberate practice is in chapter 7.) It has to be admitted, of course, that the practice may well be beneficial to the author of the review as self-promotion, and that it will likely be edifying for the residents of the culture receiving the translation because the review attracts the reading public's attention – if only in a tangential way – to the phenomenon of translation – be it of some major works of verbal art or faddish pulp fiction.

James Wood, the famous literary critic and novelist, is just one example of this aesthetic trend in specious translation analysis.[24] I will briefly consider just one example. Wood's piece in *The New York Review of Books* (2010), entitled "In a Spa

---

[22] See Venuti, Lawrence. "Towards a Translation Culture." *The Iowa Review*, September 21, 2011: // http://iowareview.uiowa.edu/page/towards_a_translation_culture (last accessed January 20, 2014).

[23] Op. cit.

[24] Here I do not at all mean any criticism of Wood's accomplishments as a literary critic and cultural commentator. I am dealing here only with the way he comments about *translations* of literary texts.

Town", is a review of the most recent translation of Mikhail Lermontov's classic *A Hero of Our Time* by Natasha Randall. Not to put too fine a point on it, it is not so much a review of a translation as a review of Lermontov's classic as if it had just been written in English. It is as if the reviewer had used the pretext of the new translation in order to set forth some of his views on this novel and to introduce it to English-language readers for the first time. In other words, in his review, James Wood, whom I respect as a literary critic and essayist, seems to confuse plain vanilla literary criticism with comparative translation criticism, which, from my perspective, should involve at least some contrastive semantic, syntactic, and pragmatic analyses of both original and translation and should also, ideally, at least mention, in a comparative kind of way, the other existing translations of the same original. What we get from James Wood by way of comments on the translation is just one brief passage – misleading and enigmatic to anyone familiar with Lermontov's text and its several translations:

> Natasha Randall's English, in her new translation, has exactly the right degree of loose velocity – this sounds like someone taking notes, patching it together as he goes along and unable to make up his mind. (Nabokov's version, the best-known older translation, is a bit more demure than Randall's, less savage.) So Pechorin, in this account, is both strongly male and slightly effeminate, bold and weak, fair and dark, finely dressed yet dusty from travel. On the one hand, the narrator is a confident 19th-century analyst, conventionally reading the body as a moral map: a man who does not swing his arms is clearly secretive. On the other, he does not want us to set any store by such observations. He is also frank about his role as a maker who touches things up: he is obviously painting a romantic "portrait" (Wood 2010).

All of that is well and good, but how does it relate to the actual original text in Russian? I personally have a number of specific questions about Wood's comments, namely: What exactly is "loose velocity," how does it manifest itself in Lermontov's text, and how would one measure it? How exactly is Randall's translation less demure and more savage than that by Nabokov? I could go on with my questions, but my point must be clear: this is not a translation review, this is literary criticism, tenuously related to the Russian original – what Venuti calls "belletrism."[25]

In contrast to Wood, a radically different tack is taken by the educator, translator, and translation critic Timothy Sergay. In his published paper presented at

---

[25] Op. cit.

the 48th annual meeting of the Southern Conference on Slavic Studies (March 25-27, 2010), Sergay simultaneously engaged four translations of *A Hero of Our Time*: those by Nabokov, Foote, Schwartz, and Randall. While admitting their general acceptability as translation variants, he points out some obvious (to a bilingual professional translator and translation critic) mistranslations or "garblings" (as Sergay prefers to put it) scattered throughout the four texts. Sergay concludes that "the cumulative effect of such garblings for readers is almost certainly a misleading impression of mystery and incoherence. There appears to be greater 'signal loss' in recent 'remasterings' of *Hero of Our Time* than there was in the previous versions of this novel that the English-speaking world already had on its shelves. The errors are all understandable ones for Anglophone students of Russian, but they are not excusable in authoritative retranslations of a well-annotated classic" (Sergay 2011: 45).

To give the reader a taste of Sergay's mode of translation analysis, here are two fragments of the table that he used in his paper to drive his points home:

Original Russian	Nabokov, 1958	Foote, 1966, Rev. 2001	Schwartz, 2004	Randall, 2009
Будет и того, что болезнь указана, а как ее излечить — это уж бог знает!	Suffice it that the disease has been pointed out; goodness knows how to cure it. (2)	Let it suffice that the malady has been diagnosed — heaven alone knows how to cure it! (4)	We will find that the disease has been diagnosed, but how one is to cure it—God only knows! (4)	[No translation]

The table above compares the translations of the last sentence in Lermontov's introduction of the main body of his book. Sergay says, "This final and crucial sentence in Lermontov's introduction is entirely omitted in Natasha Randall's translation. Her 'Foreword' simply ends on the preceding sentence, from which the words '*i vashemu*' ('and *your* misfortune as well') were likewise omitted. This same sentence is garbled by Marian Schwartz, who did not recognize the construction '*budet i togo, chto...*' as synonymous with '*khvatit i togo, chto...*' and construed it as '*budet to, chto...*': 'We will find that the disease has been diagnosed....'" (Sergay 2011: 44)

Original Russian	Nabokov, 1958	Foote, 1966, Rev. 2001	Schwartz, 2004	Randall, 2009
Хорошенькая княжна обернулась и подарила оратора долгим любопытным взором. Выражение этого взора было очень неопределенно, но не насмешливо, с чем я внутренно от души его поздравил.	The pretty young princess turned her head and bestowed a long curious glance upon the orator. The expression of this glance was very indefinite, but it was not derisive, a fact on which I inwardly congratulated him with all my heart. (87)	The pretty young princess turned and bestowed a long, curious look on the speech-maker. The feeling conveyed in her look was very hard to define, but it wasn't scorn — on which I felt Grushnitsky was to be warmly congratulated. (75)	The pretty young princess turned around and bestowed upon the orator a long, curious gaze. The expression of this gaze was rather vague, *but amused,* for which I privately congratulated *her* in all sincerity. (80)	The pretty princess turned around and gifted the orator with a long and curious gaze. The expression of this gaze was very ambiguous but not mocking, for which I applauded *her* from my innermost soul. (80, italics in final columns mine [Sergay's])

With regard to this second table, Sergay's analysis goes as follows:

> To my ear, the construction "*to gift* somebody with something" sounds like strictly legal language for the conveyance of funds and property. Here I appear to be a "conservative" in Paul Brian's book *Common Errors in English Usage:* 'Conservatives are annoyed by the use of "gift" as a verb. If the ad says "gift her with jewelry this Valentine's Day," she might prefer that you give it to her.'[26] The Russian construction '*darit'/podarit' kogo chem*' as opposed to '*darit'/podarit' komu chto*' is archaic to begin with (Evgen'eva, *Malyi akademicheskii slovar'*); Randall's predecessors did well to handle it with the elevated '*bestow upon,*' while Randall's choice of '*gifted* the orator' creates unwelcome associations with today's legal and advertising jargon. Far worse, however, is the complete garbling of the sense of the final clause of this sentence. Why should Pechorin applaud or congratulate *the princess* for the momentary seriousness of her regard for his rival, Grushnitsky, whom he holds

---

[26] See http://www.wsu.edu/~brians/errors/gift.html (last accessed January 20, 2014).

in polite contempt at this point? Mistaking *ego*, 'him,' for *eë*, 'her,' is of course an elementary error. Again, this same error is committed by Marian Schwartz, who also misconstrued 'no ne nasmeshlivo,' 'but not mocking,' as something like 'no rassmeshënnoe' and translated it as 'but amused'" (Sergay 2011: 44-45).

I believe that it is such minute dissections – or "deconstructions" – of the text at different levels of analysis (semantic, syntactic, and pragmatic) that should form part of the foundation for an informed view of how a translated text works with reference to its original. Wood's review evinces what Venuti calls a "belletristic approach" to translation criticism, whereby the critic "assigns it [a translation] an aesthetic autonomy from the source text and judges it not according to a concept of equivalence, but according to the 'standards' by which he judges original compositions. […] this approach [is] belletristic because it emphasizes aesthetic qualities of the translated text itself. It is also impressionistic in the sense that it is vague or ill-defined" (Venuti 2011).[27] Sergay's approach is an example of what Sergay and I call a "comparative translation variance analysis."[28] I treat this term as a synonym for "comparative translation discourse analysis," although the latter concept is a more comprehensive one, owing to its sociolinguistic and sociocultural dimensions.

---

[27] Venuti, Lawrence. "Towards a Translation Culture." *The Iowa Review*, September 21, 2011: // http://iowareview.uiowa.edu/page/towards_a_translation_culture (last accessed January 20, 2014).

[28] See Burak and Sergay. "Translations, Retranslations, and Multiple Translations: A Case for Translation Variance Studies." *Russian Language Journal* (RLJ). Volume 61 (2011): 3-4.

Part Two. What it Takes to be a Translator

Chapter 7

Professionals and Experts

"Translator" is a vague term that may designate a variety of categories of people involved with foreign languages and translation. First, a translator is somebody who does written translation, and an interpreter is somebody who does oral translation (consecutive, simultaneous, liaison, sight, etc.). It is mostly "written" literary translation that I am concerned with in this book. In this particular chapter, I look at what it takes to develop a high level of translation skills, or professional level of expertise.

In the translation studies literature, one comes across several vaguely-defined categories relating to the competence of people involved with doing translations: naïve translators, novice translators, semi-professionals, bilinguals, professionals, and expert translators. Defining specific categories is problematic as there are relatively few comparable human subjects that could be investigated to reach statistically valid conclusions. Gregory Shreve and Erik Angelone are among the pioneers of such investigations, and they admit that

> [...] to date, many comparative studies of cognitive processing in novices and professionals have been problematic. The participant categories have been ill-defined and have compared a variety of non-professionals, such as language students, students of translation, or non-translating bilinguals, with a host of vaguely defined "professionals" and "experts" that range from third-year advanced translation students to authentic masters of their craft (Shreve and Angelone 2010: 9).

In this chapter I will give my own definition of what it takes to be a highly skilled translator of fiction prose – an "expert professional" – with regard to his or her training, particular translation competencies, and the aspects of the "translatorial cultural other" that such an expert professional should be expected to cope with.

Riitta Jääskeläinen, a professor at the University of Joensuu, Finland, whose research focuses on the empirical study of translation processes, has been trying to answer the question "Are all professionals experts?" Her research has produced definitions of several categories of translators that shed some light on the problem of what is what and who is who in the translating business. The initial categories of subjects in translation process studies were *naïve translators* – language students who never studied translation as an academic subject, *novice translators* – language students who have had some translation training, and those who were supposed to be *professional translators*. The intuitive definition of a professional translator is somebody who has been doing translation for a living and/or has been doing it for a long time. However, experiments have produced some unexpected results. In particular, after some supposedly professional translators were subjected to experimental tests using the latest techniques of think-aloud-protocols (TAP's), computer key-stroke logging, and eye-tracking, alongside qualitative assessments of the target texts that the translators produced, "one of the unexpected findings was that sometimes translation students or inexperienced bilinguals succeeded at the experimental task, while those deemed professional translators failed at it" (Jääskeläinen 2010: 214). This has led to refining the concept of translation professionalism by combining it with the concept of expertise.

The problem of expertise has been actively studied by Anthony Pym, Neil Charness, and Anders Ericsson, to name just some of the leading researchers in this field. Expertise is generally defined as "the possession of a large body of knowledge and procedural skill" (Jääskeläinen 2010: 217) that manifest themselves "as consistently superior performance in a domain" (Jääskeläinen 2010: 215). In our case, this domain is translation of fiction prose. Specifying the distinction between professionalism in laymen's terms and expertise in terms of cognitive translation studies leads us to the conclusion that all experts are professionals, but not all self-professed or generally recognized professionals are experts. Terminologically, it will serve my present purposes to distinguish between "expert professionals" (top-notch translators of complex fiction) and semi-professionals or "just professionals," meaning those who turn out reliably adequate (workmanlike) translations but are not likely or are less equipped to venture beyond the familiar, routine methods of resolving translation problems. That is to say, such translators generally lack "adaptive expertise" – an ability to resolve novel problems and develop new conceptual understanding of their domain.

Expertise is not a direct function of the time spent doing translations. "The development of expertise requires deliberate practice, meaning "regular engagement in specific activities directed at performance enhancement" (Shreve 2006: 29)" (Jääskeläinen 2010: 217). "Deliberate practice needs to meet certain criteria, including appropriate difficulty and informative feedback (Shreve 2006)" (Jääskeläinen 2010: 217). According to Jääskeläinen and other expertise researchers, developing translation expertise requires "at least ten years or 10,000 hours of experience" (217), and that beyond the standard term of a language and translation course of studies. This is also known as the "ten-year rule." As university students of translation and interpreting in Moscow way back when, my classmates and I kept being reminded by our professors that we would only achieve a decent level of English language proficiency ten years after graduation. History has confirmed this prediction: it was only ten years after graduating and having worked as an English language instructor and interpreter and translator that I began to truly feel comfortable and confident in what I was doing.

As was mentioned earlier, studying translation expertise is not as easy as it may seem at first glance. So far, "research into translation expertise has focused on *relative expertise* [my italics], i.e., there are no studies of exceptionally talented translators" (217). And it is quite understandable. Given the difficulty and the delicate nature of naming the best translators, as well as the fact that such translators would be very few and far between, any quantitative and statistically-satisfying methods of producing representative samples for studying top professional expertise are problematic. This leaves us with the option of making mostly qualitative assessments of some translators' products and translators' own evaluations of themselves and one another, based on which we can try to work out "an ideal type" of a literary translator, equipped to deal with the composite cross-cultural "other." But first it is necessary to define translation competence, or, rather, competences.

It is generally agreed that a translator should have (1) linguistic knowledge, (2) textual knowledge, (3) transfer knowledge, (4) subject knowledge, and (5) information retrieval and management knowledge. Linguistic knowledge requires the ability to decode (understand in the minutest detail) the source text and to encode it (re-express it) as the target text. In layman's terms, the translator should know the pair of languages he or she is translating into and out of extremely well. But it is not just "being fluent" or "being a good linguist" in a foreign language in the vague American sense, meaning being able to read and speak a foreign language with widely varying degrees of proficiency. What is required is a deep knowledge of the grammar, lexicology, functional stylistics, and respective cultures of the particular pair of languages between which translation is carried out. This "static" knowledge has to be accompanied by a superior level of proficiency in the four "dynamic," or, to use a special term, performative (procedural), skills in the two languages, namely: reading, writing, listening comprehension, and speaking, even if the translator does only translations of narrative fiction, because even this kind of translator has to be finely attuned to the rhythm and flow of the narrative under translation. If a would-be translator has difficulty understanding and formulating complex and subtle thoughts in the pair of the languages he or she would like to translate between, then attempting serious translation, especially "artistic" literary translation, is premature. The two languages and cultures must first be mastered in all their complexity. In other words, the translator has to have a superior command of the two languages and cultures s/he is working in.

What happens in real life instead is that we have a large group of people who translate but do not really possess sufficient linguistic knowledge, skills, and cross-cultural awareness to do so. To me, especially suspect are people with a "half-baked" knowledge of and modest skills in several languages, who think nothing of translating from a number of languages. Again, I am talking here about translation as a "high art," or translation of complex narrative prose. What is unfortunate for subtle cross-cultural exchanges is that "literary translation into English is for the most part done by amateurs" (Bellos 2011: 29). For my part, I can add that the same is true of most translating done from English into Russian, although, generally speaking, the Russian understanding of linguistic proficiency is far more rigorous and nuanced than the American. That is as far as linguistic knowledge is concerned.

Another important characteristic of a bona fide translator is textual knowledge. Textual knowledge is the knowledge of how different types of texts are created by means of different styles and genres, and how particular styles and genres correlate in the pair of languages between which translation is carried out. The constitutive principles of textuality are well-defined in the relevant literature so I will just confine myself to saying that a text is usually characterized by its cohesion, coherence, informativity, intentionality, acceptability, situationality, and intertextuality (see Beaugrande and Dressler 1981). The translator must be in a position to interpret the text from any of those conceptual perspectives.

The translator must possess transfer competence, which is the ability to use translation techniques and strategies involving conceptual, structural and pragmatic transformations at the lexical, sentential, and text levels. This requires deliberate, focused training in the theory and practice of translation.

Subject knowledge involves an understanding of at least the key concepts and their interconnections in a particular field of knowledge. In translating fiction prose, subject knowledge means knowing the authorial style of expression and how it differs from the general usage of the source language; "hearing" the polyphony of the narrative piece (being able to discern the interactions between different characters' voices and points of view); and being able to place a particular verbal artifact (work of verbal art) within the sociocultural and political contexts of its creation and reception.

Finally, the translator should not only be aware of the relevant print and electronic reference materials, but also be efficient in doing online research, using, for example, the Russian National Corpus,[29] the Corpus of Contemporary American English (COCA),[30] the British National Corpus (BNC),[31] various translators' blogs, etc.

From the perspective of deliberate practice and translator's special competences, "even the long-time translator with twenty, thirty or more years of experience translating may not develop expertise and be capable of producing translations that exemplify 'superior performance'" (Shreve 2002: 157). Given current research, I think it is useful to differentiate between professionals and expert professionals.

Achieving the status of expert professionalism may sound like a daunting proposition but there is a way to compensate for the uneven development of translation competences in a single person. The solution is in teaming up with a kind of cross-cultural double, a kind of cross-cultural "doppelganger," a mirror image of oneself. One of the two translators would have be a native speaker of, say, Russian, a trained linguist, highly proficient in a foreign language, say, English, a trained English-to-Russian and vice versa translator/interpreter, and an expert on cross-cultural communication with a native grounding in, say, Russian culture. The other translator would have to be a mirror image of the first – a native speaker of English, a linguist proficient in Russian, a trained translator/interpreter from Russian into English and vice versa, and an expert on cross-cultural communication with a native grounding, say, in American culture. A perfect mutually complementary pair will be problematic, but attempting such paired collaboration would go a long way to eliminating language, and cultural errors and misunderstandings.

There are some successful examples of collaborative translations approximating the model I have outlined. These are Richard Pevear and Larissa Volokhonsky, the husband-and-wife team that has translated a large amount of Russian fiction today, and also Richard Chandler, the British translator, who often

[29] http://www.ruscorpora.ru/en/index.html

[30] http://corpus.byu.edu/coca/x.asp?w=960&h=540

[31] http://www.natcorp.ox.ac.uk/

works in collaboration with his wife Elizabeth and sometimes with two or three other of his colleagues (Olga Meerson, Angela Livingstone, Nadya Bourova, and Eric Naiman). In addition to that, Chandler often engages in "crowdsourcing" by going public with his questions on the Slavists' listserv SEELANGS. This brings its results: Robert Chandler's translations are widely held in high esteem.

Bilinguals are a special case. But even in the case of the relatively rare completely bilingual person, to work in translation such a person would still need to have formal linguistic expertise, be trained in translation, and have a discerning understanding of the two cultures in order to translate with confidence and effectively.

To sum up, an expert professional translator should be bilingual or near-bilingual through birth, education, and immersion in the two cultures. This is someone possessed of "dual cognitive abilities" – parallel concept-processing brain capacities and thinking tracks. Indeed, the latest cognitive research suggests that "proficient bilinguals can access concepts directly from the second language without having to perform an internal translation via the first language. Expertise studies indicate that the advancement of proficiency is accompanied, most likely, by distinct changes in the way the bilingual brain is organized" (Diamond and Shreve 2002: 301).

An expert translator in all of the above senses of the term is a rare species indeed. It would seem that such a person is doubly cognitively and eruditionally equipped as compared with the creator of the original text. This "cognitive bifurcation" is evidenced when a bilingual or near-bilingual cannot translate his or her own texts accurately – they can only reconceptualize, if ever so slightly, and rewrite them anew, thus creating parallel originals. A famous example is Nabokov, who could not really translate his own works – he rewrote them. Milan Kundera and Jacque Derrida also seem to be a case in point. As Theo Hermans points out, "For some authors self-translation proves an impossible task [...], despite prodigious linguistic skill" (Hermans 2007: 20-21). I myself cannot translate my own articles from English into Russian and vice versa. When I write or speak in English or Russian, it is as if a mental switch is flipped, tapping me into a different conceptual matrix and chain of associations. When teaching, it is also much easier for me to use English or Russian throughout the class, without switching between them. In mixed and linguistically less proficient classes, I have to switch between languages all the time, and after two periods of teaching I feel emotionally drained. This does not happen when I operate in just one language. The old saying "to have another language is to possess a second soul" seems more than just a metaphor.

Chapter 8

Two Famous Translators' Perspectives on the Translator's "Other Souls"

To avoid being suspected of banal generalizations, I will resort to an extended quote on the subject of what it takes to be an expert translator from a testimony by the already mentioned – very much "real life" – famous British Russian-to-English translator Robert Chandler. In his 2010 interview with SRAS (The School of Russian and Asian Studies), Robert Chandler talks about his team's retranslation (after an almost 15-year interval) of their own translation of Andrey Platonov's classic *The Foundation Pit*, which is a supremely intricate and treacherous text. Chandler has the following conception of an ideal translator:

> The ideal translator of Platonov would be bilingual and have an encyclopedic knowledge of Soviet life. He would be able to detect buried allusions not only to the classics of Russian and European literature, but also to speeches of Stalin, to articles by such varied figures as Bertrand Russell and Anatoly Lunacharsky (the first Bolshevik Commissar for Enlightenment), to copies of *Pravda* from the 1930s and to long-forgotten works of Soviet literature. He would be familiar with Soviet-speak, with the rituals and language of Russian Orthodoxy, with everyday details of Russian peasant life, with the terminology of mechanical and electrical engineering, and with the digging of wells and the operation of steam locomotives. This imaginary translator would also be a gifted and subtle punster. Most important of all, his ear for English speech patterns would be so fine that he could maintain the illusion of a speaking voice, or voices, even while the narrator or the individual characters are using extraordinary language or expressing extraordinary thoughts. Much has been written about Platonov's creativity and language; not enough has been written about the subtlety with which – even in narrative – he reproduces the music of speech, its shifts of intonation and rhythm. If Platonov's command of tone and idiom were less than perfect, his infringements of linguistic norms would by now seem self-conscious and dated. In short, Platonov is a poet, and almost every line of his finest work poses problems for a translator. A perfect translation, like the original, would sound not only extraordinary and shocking, but also – in some indefinable way – right and natural. And so … I realized long ago that the only way to go about the task of translating Platonov was to find collaborators.

One indication of how deeply many Russian writers and critics admire Platonov is the extent of their generosity to the translators; I now have a large list of people I can turn to for help. Above all, I have the good fortune to have as my closest collaborators my wife, who shares my love of Platonov, and the brilliant American scholar, Olga Meerson. Olga was brought up in the Soviet Union, she knows a great deal about Russian Orthodoxy, she has written a brilliant book about Platonov and she has the sensitive ear of someone who once trained as a professional violinist. She has deepened our understanding of almost every sentence of *Soul* and *The Foundation Pit*. Our new translation[32] is, by the way, an entirely new translation – not merely a revision of the translation we did for *Harvill* in 1994 (sic).[33] There are passages in the first translation that I still like, but at the time we were working in the dark, with little contact with Russian scholars. The new translation, on the other hand, is – I believe – the product of at least some degree of understanding. No other work of literature, by the way, means so much to me that I have wanted to translate it twice! (Chandler 2010).

The American translator Anne Fisher is another example of how long and what it takes to be able to translate complex prose fiction. Among other writers, Fisher has translated Il'f and Petrov – the two famous Soviet prose authors of the 1920s and 1930s that worked as a team. Prior to translating their *The Twelve Chairs*[34] and *The Little Golden Calf*,[35] Fisher had written her PhD dissertation on the two novels and collaborated with Il'f's daughter, Aleksandra Il'f, on a biography of Il'f and a translation of his notebooks. Apart from her expert background knowledge of her translation subject, Fisher relies on the Internet, reference materials, and a little help from her friends. Here is part of what she shared with Josh Wilson in her interview for SRAS:

> I find myself using the Internet for English more than I would have thought, checking to make sure that something really is commonly said in English, and

---

[32] Platonov, Andrey. *The Foundation Pit*. (A new translation from the definitive Russian text by Robert & Elizabeth Chandler and Olga Meerson.) New York, NY: New York Review Books, 2009.

[33] Platonov, Andrey. *The Foundation Pit*. Translated by Robert Chandler and Geoffrey Smith. London: The Harvill Press, 1996.

[34] Ilf, Ilya and Petrov, Evgeny. *The Twelve Chairs*. Translated by Anne O. Fisher. Evanston, IL: Northwestern University Press, 2011.

[35] Ilf, Ilya & Petrov, Evgeny. *The Little Golden Calf*. Translated by Anne O. Fisher. Montpelier, VT: Russian Life Books, 2009. A competing translation by Konstantin Gurevich and Helen Andersen with the title *The Golden Calf* came out the same year (Rochester, NY: Open Letter).

that I don't just make it up. And it's always worth your while to take the extra time to flip through a thesaurus, too […]. With *The Little Golden Calf* I was lucky enough to have both an editor and a copyeditor who are Russian to English translators themselves, so we had some important discussions that made the translation stronger […]. Finally, there's also the question of having enough friends. Russians say "ne imei sto rublei, a imei sto druzei" (literally: don't have a hundred rubles, but rather a hundred friends), and they are totally right! I rely liberally on people who know more than I do […] (Fisher 2010).

The conclusion from the above two interviews is that an expert translator has to be a person of great erudition, but also a person who understands his or her educational and cultural limitations. Such a person has to engage with other – no less and less erudite – minds, including the author of the work being translated, if at all possible.

From my own life experience, I am certain that a true artist and master of translation can only work with maximum effect within the realm of only a pair of languages or three at the most. Again, I am talking here about translating complex, subtle, imaginatively original narrative fiction. Alas, there is too much hackwork out in the translation world produced by well-meaning, overconfident people blithely translating from several languages.

Chapter 9

A Famous Writer as a "Translator"

In an article entitled "Found in Translation",[36] the famous American author Michael Cunnigham looks at some "invisible" aspects of literary translation from the point of view of a writer whose works get translated into many languages and who has a rich experience of interacting with the translators of his works. His article is a concise explication of translation as a process of tripartite artistic interaction and creation. Here is Cunnigham's opening paragraph:

As the author of "Las Horas," "Die Stunden" and "De Uren" – ostensibly the Spanish, German and Dutch translations of my book "The Hours," but actually *unique works in their own right* [my italics] – I've come to understand that all literature is a product of translation. That is, translation is not merely a job assigned to a translator expert in a foreign language, but a long, complex and even profound series of transformations that involve the writer and reader as well. "Translation" as a human act is, like so many human acts, a far more complicated proposition than it may initially seem to be (Cunnigham 2010).

Cunnigham then goes on to explain how he interacts with translators:

I encourage the translators of my books to take as much license as they feel that they need. This is not quite the heroic gesture it might seem, because I've learned, from working with translators over the years, that the original novel is, in a way, a translation itself. It is not, of course, translated into another language but it is a translation from the images in the author's mind to that which he is able to put down on paper. Here's a secret. Many novelists, if they are pressed and if they are being honest, will admit that the finished book is a rather rough translation of the book they'd intended to write. It's one of the heartbreaks of writing fiction. You have, for months or years, been walking around with the idea of a novel in your mind, and in your mind it's transcendent, it's brilliantly comic and howlingly tragic, it contains everything you know, and everything you can imagine, about human life on the planet

---

[36] Cunningham, Michael. "Found in Translation." *The New York Times*, October 2, 2010. Retrieved on October 7, 2010 from www.nytimes.com/2010/10/03/opinion/03cunningham.html?_r=1&scp=3&sq=michael%20cunningham&st=c-s-e

earth. It is vast and mysterious and awe-inspiring. It is a cathedral made of fire. But even if the book in question turns out fairly well, it's never the book that you'd hoped to write. It's smaller than the book you'd hoped to write. It is an object, a collection of sentences, and it does not remotely resemble a cathedral made of fire. It feels, in short, like a rather inept translation of a mythical great work. The translator, then, is simply moving the book another step along the translation continuum. The translator is translating a translation. A translator is also translating a work in progress, one that has a beginning, middle and end but is not exactly finished, even though it's being published. A novel, any novel, if it's any good, is not only a slightly disappointing translation of the novelist's grandest intentions, it is also the most finished draft he could come up with before he collapsed from exhaustion (ibid.).

The process of translation does not finish with the translator's final period in the text. The translation continues in the minds of its cross-cultural readers. This is the stage of a text's life that an expert translator always keeps at the front of his or her mind. Anticipating the readers' reaction and making assumptions about the readers' cultural background are aspects of translation referred to in the profession as "pragmatics." Cunningham has this to say about the receivers of a translation:

Writing [...] does not exist without an active, consenting reader. Writing requires a different level of participation. Words on paper are abstractions, and everyone who reads words on paper brings to them a different set of associations and images. What the reader is doing, then, is translating the words on the pages into his or her own private, imaginary lexicon, according to his or her interests and needs and levels of comprehension (ibid.).

The reader's "interests, needs and levels of comprehension" as perceived by the translator are also a dimension of the translated text. At the end of his article Cunnigham summarizes how this tripartite, holy – or otherwise – alliance functions:

Here, then, is the full process of translation. At one point we have a writer in a room, struggling to approximate the impossible vision that hovers over his head. He finishes it, with misgivings. Some time later we have a translator struggling to approximate the vision, not to mention the particulars of language and voice, of the text that lies before him. He does the best he can, but is never satisfied. And then, finally, we have the reader. The reader is the least tortured of this trio, but the reader too may very well feel that he is missing something in the book, that through sheer ineptitude he is failing to be a proper vessel for the book's overarching vision (ibid.).

Cunnigham does not separate the three entities, for him they constitute a continuous loop of creative search for perfection:

> We are on a quest, and are not discouraged by our collective suspicion that the perfection we look for in art is about as likely to turn up as is the Holy Grail. That is one of the reasons we, I mean we humans, are not only the creators, translators and consumers of literature, but also its subjects (ibid.).

And so the eternal quest continues.

Chapter 10

A Translator's Ethics and "Verbal Overshadowing"

Why and how do you retranslate a translation? There may be three kinds of translation ethics applicable in three different situations.

Scenario number one: You translate something that you have an overwhelming desire to translate because you are deeply enamored of the text, its author, and the culture in which it was created. You do not care that the text has already been translated, perhaps several times. You never refer to the existing translations while you are creating your version of a translation. Then you start evaluating your translation while looking at different other translations. The idea of taking your translation to a publisher never enters your head. You keep your translation in a safe place, away from public scrutiny. Maybe for your kids, or a restricted circle of friends. This scenario belongs in the realm of fantasy.

Scenario number two: Having translated a precious text and before you even touch any of the previous translations, you try to convince a publisher, solely on the basis of the perceived merits of your translation (for which it would be difficult to make a convincing case without a scrupulous comparative analysis of the original and your translation), your reputation and connections that s/he should publish it. The awkward question "How is your translation different/'better' from the previous one/s?" is bound to arise. Your response, "I never compared my translation with the previous translation/s. And that is its uniqueness." In the highly unlikely event that you get past a publisher, your translation gets accepted and published. Now you start comparing it with the ones that came before yours, and, most likely, begin to fall into alternating states of elation and depression – a state of "depration," so to speak, i.e. a mixed state when you feel happy that your translation has been published (your righteous professionalism has been vindicated and your sense of vanity satisfied) but at the same time realize that, in some respects, the previous translation/s are superior to yours. That is, even from your own personal, subjective perspective. Unless you have a tight hold on the publisher or a controlling stake in the publishing company, this scenario also belongs in the realm of fantasy – O.K., maybe, magical realism.

Scenario number three (the Pevear and Volokhonsky phenomenon): You use all the existing translations of one source text and rework them into an edited "compiled" – hopefully, improved – translation of your own. In this case your translation is the result of an *in absentia* collaborative effort together with the previous translators (dead and living ones), i.e., you are not the sole translator who has produced an improved version of the original, but a coauthor of all the other translators whose translations you consulted, even if your translation is deemed – by whoever cares to assess it – superior to the ones that came before yours. Translation history shows, however, that cases of such attributions are next to non-existent. So this scenario is also at least partially fantastic. But this last scenario is also problematic. It is problematic because for a linguist, whose habitat is various texts, even a cursory look at a text, especially a rival text, leaves an indelible trace or imprint on the mind, which, in one way or another, will be reflected in the similar text s/he is producing. The unbearable inescapability of being influenced by a text is every translator's or writer's occupational hazard – an anxiety of influence, in Harold Bloom's terms. In translation, this "verbal overshadowing" is particularly haunting because it derives from the very same texts that you intend to replicate in your own way.

It is only people who remember and perceive networks of linguistic and cultural connections through words, idioms, and texts. Texts have no memory or perception of their own but they do carry the residual imprints of their translators. These imprints are determined by the translator's worldview, education, and understanding and interpretation of the source text, which in turn become reflected and refracted – if only in subtle and barely detectable ways – in the target text. There is no way a re-translator can get away from "the other translator's shadow." It seems to me that in order to be completely honest with oneself, in cases of retranslation, one should emulate the translators of the King James Bible who thought of themselves as revisers, not creators of a new translation (see Norton 2011: 7). In their preface, "The Translators to the Reader", they say:

> Truly, good Christian reader, we never thought from the beginning that we should need to make a new translation, nor yet to make of a bad one a good one…but to make a good one better, or out of many good ones one principal good one […]" (Norton 2011: 7).

I think that in some present-day cases of retranslations it would be fair and ethical to make similar disclaimers.

Chapter 11

Russian Translators Interviewed

The literary translation sociologist Elena Kalashnikova's 2008 book *Po-russki s liubov'iu: Besedy s perevodchikami* is the first comprehensive survey of the Russian translation scene undertaken in recent years. *Po-russki s liubov'iu* is a unique collection of 87 interviews that Elena Kalashnikova conducted from 2000 to 2006 with Russian literary translators working out of a wide range of languages into Russian. The first striking fact that emerged from Kalashnikova's survey is that the majority of the "professional" translators have never been formally trained as translators: for most of them, translation is a labor of love, with means for everyday existence being obtained from other sources.

The interviewees expressed some unconventional opinions on translation theory and practice. Here is my concretized summary of the main motifs permeating the interviews. Do male and female translators translate differently? – They usually do, with women, supposedly, feeling the "intonation" of the text better than men. On the whole, the differences, though felt, seem to be hard to pinpoint, with the concept "intonation" remaining undefined. What are the advantages of using interlinear (word-for-word) translations of poetry to produce "poetic" translations? – Interlinear translations preserve the original imagery and metaphoricity and may push the translator's imagination in unusual directions. Why do young people seem to prefer more literalist, word-for-word translations that at times strain standard Russian usage? – Because young people like things that do not read like a high school textbook, especially given their general idealization of global culture (gadgetry, music, videos and so forth), and, last but not least, the fact that the Internet lexicon and style are now affecting about 70 million Russians (out of a total of 142.5 million),[37] most of them young. Which particular texts are virtually untranslatable? – Complex poetry that plays on subtle shades of meaning and culture-specific allusions. In poetry the form is the message, and much of it cannot resonate with the culturally alien readers the way it does with the source audience. How can reading your prose translation out loud be helpful in improving it? – It makes the translator hear the prosody of the original text better, which may help reproduce it better in translation, if only partially. Can you assess the quality of a translation without

---

[37] http://www.bbc.co.uk/russian/rolling_news/2011/12/111226_rn_russia_internet_users.shtml

comparing it with the original? – It seems that you can – in some cases. If the translation makes for a compelling reading, there is a good chance that that is because the translator did a good job, or "too good a job," the way of Irinarkh Vvedenskii[38] did. In my estimate, this rule-of-thumb assessment is confirmed in about 60 percent of cases, but one has to take the trouble to compare translation and original anyway. Without a close comparison the impression is just that – an impression. Is the translator's task more complicated than that of the author of the original text? – Kalashnikova never asked this question. I do. And my answer is yes.

The recurrent complaints of the translators in Kalashnikova's survey were that they were outrageously underpaid and had to work to truly unrealistic deadlines. In the words of Kirill Medvedev, "[...] translators have the psychology of the 'little person.' Each work they translate becomes [Akakii Akakievich's] overcoat for them" (Kalashnikova 2008: 338). Many interviewees lamented that, for the general public, translators continue to be invisible, being somewhat "like cesspool cleaners – you don't know they exist until you have a sewage-disposal problem" (Kalashnikova/Silakova 2008: 444).

Some of the older translators interviewed by Kalashnikova were upset at the loss of the cultural status that literary translation enjoyed in the Soviet times when it was a well-institutionalized, state-supported profession generally equated with refined artistic activity or high art. My sense today is that – after a hiatus roughly corresponding to the periods of *perestroika* of the late 1980s, the wild 1990s, and the early 2000s – the understanding among the general public that translation is a highly sophisticated activity is beginning to be slowly revived. What remains unresolved, though, is the problem of the erosion of the once generally well-institutionalized stringent criteria for assessing the quality of translation. And I cannot see any socioeconomic incentives for the commissioners of translations and/or their publishers to resolve it in the near future. Nor do I see any prospects of increased pay for translators' work any time soon. However, amid the chorus of lamentations about the disintegration of the Russian-Soviet school of translation (epitomized by the Kashkíntsy and their followers) and the general decline in the quality of literary translation, already in 2001 there were dissenting voices. One of them was that of the doyen of Russian literary translation, professor Viktor Golyshev. When asked by

---

[38] Irinarkh Ivanovich Vvedenskskii (1813-1855) was a prolific translator of English classics into Russian (Dickens, Thackeray and others) who introduced his own changes and arguably improvements into the original texts to bring them into line with what he perceived as contemporary cultural expectations of the audiences.

Kalashnikova in 2001 who he could name as interesting young translators, Golyshev said:

> I don't know any of the very young ones, but among the older ones, I would name Kuz'minskii, Dashevskii, Motylev... In general, when they talk about a decline in translation and about the erstwhile golden age, I don't agree. What decline are we talking about if, besides the people I have named, there are acting – or living and capable of acting – translators such as Kharitonov, Bespalova, Surits, Kan, Boshniak, Babkov, Bernshtein, Bogdanovskii, Kormil'tsev, Livergant... I'm sure I left three or four out. All of them are talented people, and besides, they are very different, more different than the good translators of past generations (Golyshev 2001; Kalashnikova 2008: 169).

Nine years later, in a new interview with Kalashnikova on May 12, 2010,[39] Golyshev denied any decline of translation in Russia again, adding, however, that today "only enthusiasts and wives of rich people can afford to work in translation as one cannot make a living out of it" (Kalashnikova 2010).

The poet, literary critic, publisher, and translator Ian Probshtein noted in 2004 that "[...] the institute of translation editors has virtually ceased to exist [...] and many translators have mutated from the proverbial 'post horses of enlightenment' into draft bullocks or mules in the employ of the book-producing business" (Kalashnikova 2008: 398). This has not changed: The majority of translations are submitted and accepted for publication as so-called translator-edited texts.

In the early 2000s, the rate of output and the quality of most translations, as well as the translator-publisher relationship, reminded one of the interviewees, the translator Mikhail Rudnitsky, of a Soviet-era joke about an exemplary collective farm dairymaid who had been regularly "over-fulfilling" milk production quotas. One day, still unsatisfied by the milking woman's productivity, her boss asks her pointedly, "Will you be able to produce 12,000 liters of milk [a month]?" "Yes, boss," the cow-milker replies, "But the milk will be 100 percent water" (Kalashnikova 2008: 429). My research confirms that Russian publishers continue to be satisfied with arrangements of this kind, that is to say, the translators' work-load pressure and virtual sweatshop conditions of work have not eased off.

Did Kalashnikova's interviews reveal any prevalent methodological trends in or general approaches to translation? Few of the interviewees gave her well-rounded

---

[39] http://www.youtube.com/watch?v=ETqLKJF1PNM

descriptions of their translation methodologies, usually confining themselves to discussing separate aspects of their work. Taken together, however, their comments revealed a predominantly intuitive approach to translation and the eternal vacillation of the translation pendulum between so-called "free" (*vol'nyi*) and "literalist" (*bukvalistskii*) translation. Today's discussions of translation issues online reveal – with some exceptions – a greater engagement of theory and practice, although the intuitive approach to translation practice seems to prevail.

Despite the generally intuitive cast of mind, most of the translators implicitly adhere to what may be called the presumption of explicability. In the Kalashnikova interviews, some explicit comments on this score came from Elena Kostiukovich:

> "Talking about the translation profession, we should proceed from the assumption that you're able to explain everything you do [in the translated text]. In some parts of the text, you may think it important to depart from the original – then depart and demonstrate your brilliance. In other parts of the text, be literally accurate. In still others, imitate the exact sound of the original" (Kalashnikova 2008: 279).

When asked specifically if he was a proponent of "exact" or "free" translation, Aleksandr Livergant (a longtime professor of translation studies at a major Moscow university) had this to say on the subject:

> A mathematician would call such a question fallacious. [...] Everything depends on the translator's perceptiveness and the language of the original, which in some cases lends itself to a close, literal translation and in others resists literalism. One often hears of literalist translators, but such translators simply don't know how to translate. They are either incompetent or in too much of a hurry. [...] I am confident that a good translator is sometimes a literalist and at other times, on the contrary, departs from the letter of the text. When to do the former or the latter is a question of the translator's choice, taste, and aesthetics (Kalashnikova 2008: 297-298).

Does translation theory exist? For the minority in the Kalashnikova survey that answered this question definitively, it does not: "It is an artificial construct of some [...] idlers" (Kalashnikova/Volokhonsky 2008: 133); or "It is something fictional" (Kalashnikova/Mikushevich 2008: 349). A few responded vaguely along the lines that theory does exist in the form of some general translation principles and that, in order to arrive at them, "it is necessary to determine and define the objective basis of intuition in translation, that on which it rests" (Kalashnikova/Smirnitskaia 2008: 463). However, most of the interviewees were never asked this question.

Can translation be taught? The majority seemed to think that you could not teach translation as a creative activity, – what you could teach was translation skills or strategies. Acquiring them on your own would be like reinventing the wheel, so teaching oneself to translate more or less professionally would take much longer than when you are taught formally (Kalashnikova/Golyshev 2008: 169).

Theory or no theory, "teachability" or "non-teachability" of translation, the current vibrant books and films market in Russia indicates that translations of most major English-language best sellers and voiceover dubs of blockbuster movies are released in Russia nearly simultaneously with their releases in the USA and Europe.

Given the virtual absence of systematic studies or research on translation and interpretation as a professional and cultural institution in Russia today, Kalashnikova's work may be called a truly historical document that has recorded not only the polyphony of voices of a very significant group of practicing translators talking about their individual translation practices but also – to a significant extent – the state of translation as a cultural institution in Russia in the first half-decade of the 21st century. (Unfortunately, some of the great Russian translators Kalashnikova interviewed are now dead.) My only friendly criticism is that the researcher should have stuck to a more rigorous and uniform set of questions that she asked of her interviewees. From my perspective, this might have improved the scholarly validity of the results of the interviews. But I ascribe this somewhat problematic aspect of the methodological rigor of the survey – when different questions were asked of different translators – to the pragmatics of the interview as a type of discourse and a special method of research. In any case, the translators' numerous insightful, practice-based comments scattered throughout the text of the book are certainly not only an excellent read both for the professional and the non-professional but also a treasure-trove of material for English-to-Russian and Russian-to-English advanced translation seminars.

What about today – the year 2014? Today Kalashnikova is beginning a new project focusing on the history of the Soviet school of translation, in general, and the Kashkin circle of translators, in particular. As for the most cutting-edge – or should I say "bleeding edge"? – discussions of the theory and practice of translation, I can confidently refer the reader to the Russian translators' journal *Mosty* [Мосты] and its core contributors – Buzadzhi, Ermolovich, Lanchikov and others. This quarterly journal, launched in 2004, has continued the best traditions of the Russian school of translation. *Mosty* is the present-day voice of the Russian translators. I discuss some of the key contributions of the journal to translation studies in some detail in my latest book, *"The Other" in Translation: A Case for Comparative Translation Studies* (2013).

Conclusion

The translator has to have a "multiple personality," coterminous and compatible not only with the author and the readers but also with the realistically "internalizable" totality of the linguistic and cultural material that I have briefly discussed in this book. The translator has to have a detached view of himself or herself as a product of and an agent in a particular sociocultural context. In other words, a "defamiliarization of oneself" has to be practiced at all times in the process of translating, which is only possible as a self-conscious monitoring of the multifaceted interactions of oneself with the composite and elusive "other." Chandler, Fisher, and Cunnigham provide good illustrations of how translators ought to operate, emphasizing the necessity to transcend oneself in the process of translating and evaluating the quality of translations.

Given the complexity and required erudition involved in a literary translator's work, the translator is much more than a translator – she or he is, in fact, an equal co-author of a work of fiction and an equal co-participant in cross-cultural translation discourse. In a recent publication, one of the key contributors to the *Mosty* journal,Viktor Lanchikov, has this to say about the qualities of a true high-art practicing literary translator: "The frustration and joy that the translator experiences are no weaker than the exact same feelings familiar to any creative person. Verbal inventiveness, stylistic flexibility, and a special acuity in distinguishing shades of meaning – all of these qualities are no less (and, perhaps, are even more) important in literary translation than in authorial creativity" (Lanchikov 2011, 2/30: 35).

My own experience, intuition and introspection somehow urge me to go even further than that – out on a limb, in fact – and say that, in general, an expert translator, in the senses defined in this book, may be a person that is more comprehensively equipped with regard to linguistic skills, cultural awareness, and, arguably, cognitive capacities than the author herself.[40]

Generally speaking, I believe that translation is not so much a transformation, transfer or representation of complex meaning across cultures as a re-ideation of the

---

[40] Rare exceptions are known when the author is totally bilingual and bicultural, in which case he or she will be unable to "merely" translate, but will write or rewrite a piece of narrative fiction from scratch (think Nabokov, Makine, and some other "diasporic authors"). The benefit and drawback of such a "double-linguocultural-personality syndrome" is that the author, while translating himself, will, in fact, produce a different original: the author will have reinvented or "out-originaled" the original; he or she would have "plagiarized" himself or herself.

source text by other means. In mathematical terms, this means that the potential number of translations is limitless. In practical terms, though, a limited number of (re-)translations proves sufficient.

Finally, I have to admit that, of course, my tentative "translator's cognitive superiority hypothesis" needs to be supported by serious empirical research based, among other things, on cognitive psychology and neuroscience. But given the uniqueness of the research subject and the difficulty in forming samples and extrapolating results, such research will take a while to materialize. For now I suggest that we merely have the audacity to entertain the hypothesis as a possibility.

64

(Sources Directly Quoted From and Referred To)

Adams, Douglas. *The Hitchhiker's Guide to the Galaxy*. New York: Crown
    Publishers, Inc., 1980.

Baudelaire, Charles. *Tableaux Parisiens*. Heidelberg: Verlag von Richard Wiedbach,
    1923.

Beaugrande, Alain de and Dressler, Wolfgang Ulrich. *Introduction to Text
    Linguistics*. London: Longman, 1981.

Bellos, David. *Is That a Fish in Your Ear? Translation and the Meaning of
    Everything*. New York: Faber and Faber, Inc., 2011.

Benjamin, Walter. "The Task of the Translator" in *Illuminations*. Edited by Hannah
    Arendt. New York: Schocken Books, 1968, pp. 69-82.

Berlin, Isaiah. "The Pursuit of the Ideal" in *The Proper Study of Mankind. An
    Anthology of Essays*. Edited by Henry Hardy and Roger Hausheer. New York:
    Farrar, Straus and Giroux, 1997.

Bloom, Harold. *The Anxiety of Influence. A Theory of Poetry*. New York: Oxford UP,
    1973.

Bloom, Harold. *The Western Canon: The Books and School of the Ages*. New York:
    Riverhead Books, 1994.

Bourdieu, Pierre. *Distinction: A Social Critique of the Judgement of Taste*.
    Translated by Richard Nice. London: Routledge, 1984 (French original
    completed in 1979).

Burak, A.L. *Translating Culture-2: Sentence and Paragraph Semantics. / Perevod i
    mezhkul'turnaia kommunikatsiia-2: Semantika predlozheniia I abzatsa.*
    Moskva: R.Valent, 2006, 2013.

Burak, A. L. *Translating Culture-1: Words. Perevod i mezhkul'turnaia
    kommunikatsiia -1: Slova*. Moskva: R.Valent, 2002, 2005, 2010.

Burak, A. L. *"The Other" in Translation: A Case for Comparative Translation
    Studies*. Bloomington, Indiana: Slavica, 2013.

Burak, A. L. and Sergay, Timothy. "Translations, Retranslations, and Multiple Translations: A Case for Translation Variance Studies." *Russian Language Journal* (RLJ). Volume 61 (2011): 3-4.

Buzadzhi, D. M. "Zakalka perevodom. Ob ideologicheskoi storone perevodcheskoi praktiki i prepodavaniia perevoda." ["The Crucible of Translation: Some Considerations Concerning Translation Practice and Pedagogy."] *Mosty. Zhurnal perevodchikov*. Moskva: R.Valent, No. 1/29 (2011): 55-66.

Buzadzhi, D. M. "K voprosu ob opredelenii poniatiia 'perevod'." ["On Defining Translation."] *Mosty. Zhurnal perevodchikov*. Moskva: R.Valent, No. 2/30 (2011): 44-55.

Chandler, Robert. "A Passion for Collaboration." In "To the Editor," *The New York Review of Books*. May 13, 2010, p. 69.

Chandler, Robert. "Translation as a Career and a Love." Interview with Robert Chandler by Josh Wilson. Retrieved on October 10, 2010 from: www.sras.org/robert_chandler_on_translation_as_a_career

Chukovskii, Kornei. *Vysokoe iskusstvo*. In *Kornei Chukovskii. Sobranie sochinenii v shesti tomakh. Tom tretii*. Moskva: Khudozhestvennaia literatura, 1966. 237-833.

Chukovsky, K. I. *A High Art*. Translated and edited by Lauren G. Leighton. Knoxville: The University of Tennessee Press, 1984.

Cunningham, Michael. "Found in Translation." *The New York Times*, October 2, 2010. Retrieved on October 7, 2010 from www.nytimes.com/2010/10/03/opinion/03cunningham.html?_r=1&scp=3&sq=michael%20cunningham&st=c-s-e

Denzin, N. K. and Lincoln, Y.S.(eds.) *Handbook of Qualitative Research*. Thousand Oaks: CA, 1994.

Derrida, Jacques. *Writing and Difference*. Translated by Alan Bass. Chicago: University of Chicago Press, 1967/1980.

Derrida, Jacques. *Of Grammatology*. Translated by Gayatri Chakravorty Spivak. Baltimore: Johns Hopkins University Press, 1976/1998.

Derrida, Jacques. "Living on /Border Lines." In *Deconstruction and Criticism*. Translated by J. Hulbert. New York: Continuum, 1979, pp. 75-176.

Derrida, Jacques. *Margins of Philosophy*. Translated by Alan Bass. Chicago: University of Chicago Press, 1982.

Derrida, Jacques. *Dissemination*. Translated by Barbara Johnson. Chicago: University of Chicago Press, 1983.

Derrida, Jacques. *The Ear of the Other. Texts and Discussions with Jacques Derrida. Otobiography, Transference, Translation.* English edition edited by Christie McDonald. A translation by Peggy Kamuf of the French edition edited by Claude Levesque and Christie McDonald. Lincoln: University of Nebraska Press, 1985a.

Derrida, Jacques. "Des Tours de Babel." In Graham, J. (ed.). *Difference in Translation*. Translated by J. Graham. Ithaca, New York: Cornell University Press, 1985b, pp. 165-248.

Diamond, Bruce J. and Shreve, Gregory M. "Neural and Psychological Correlates of Translation and Interpreting in the Bilingual Brain. Recent Perspectives." In *Translation and Cognition*. Ed. Gregory M. Shreve and Erik Angelone. Amsterdam/Philadelphia: John Benjamins Publishing Company, 2010. 289-321.

Dudek, Sarah. "Walter Benjamin and the Religion of Translation." *Cipher Journal*. Retrieved on July 18, 2010 from:
http://www.cipherjournal.com/html/dudek_benjamin.html

Dyson, Freeman. "Science on the Rampage." *The New York Review of Books*, April 5, 2012, 38-39.

Ermolovich, D. I., Krasavina, T. M. *New Comprehensive Russian-English Dictionary*. (Corrected and Supplemented.) Moskva: Media, 2006.

Ermolovich, D. I. "Chto mozhno sdelat' iz konfetki." [What You Can Turn a Piece of Candy Into.] *Mosty. Zhurnal perevodchikov*. Moskva: R.Valent, No. 3/19 (2008): 60-70 (http://yermolovich.ru/index/0-46).

Ermolovich, D. I. "O 'Longmane' bednom zamolvite slovo." ["Put in a Good Word for Poor 'Longman'."] *Mosty. Zhurnal perevodchikov.* Moskva: R.Valent, No. 2/22 (2009): http://yermolovich.ru/index/0-69 (Accessed on June 17, 2012.)

Ermolovich, D. I. "Kritika na sluzhbe praktiki." ["Criticism in the Service of Practice."] *Mosty. Zhurnal perevodchikov.* Moskva: R.Valent, No. 1/29 (2011): 43-44.

Ermolovich, D. I. "Slepaia vavilonskaia rybka." ["The Blind Babel Fish."] *Mosty. Zhurnal perevodchikov.* Moskva: R.Valent, No. 2/30 (2011): 56-71. (The article can also be accessed at http://yermolovich.ru/Yermolovich_Most2-30-2011.pdf).

Fisher, Anne. "Translation and Interpreting as Profession." Interview with Anne Fisher by Josh Wilson. Retrieved on October 10, 2010 from: www.sras.org/anne_fisher_translation_interpreting

Gasparov, M. "Briusov i bukvalizm." In *Poetika perevoda: sbornik statei.* Ed. S. Goncharenko. Moskva: Raduga, [1971] 1988. 29-62.

Gasparov, M. L *Zapisi i vypiski.* Moskva: Novoe literaturnoe obozrenie, 2000.

Golyshev, Viktor. "Parshivuiu knigu khorosho perevesti nel'zia." ["A Lousy Book Cannot be Translated Well."]: http://old.russ.ru/krug/20010628_kal.html (Published on June 28, 2001; accessed on May 14, 2012).

Hermans, Theo. *Translating Others. Volume 1.* London and New York: Routledge, 2007.

Ilf, Ilya & Petrov, Evgeny. *The Little Golden Calf.* Translated by Anne O. Fisher. Montpelier, VT: Russian Life Books, 2009.

Ilf, Ilya and Petrov Evgeny. *The Golden Calf.* Translated from the Russian by Konstantin Gurevich and Helen Anderson. Rochester, NY: Open Letter, 2009.

Ilf, Ilya and Petrov, Evgeny. *The Twelve Chairs.* Translated by Anne O. Fisher. Evanston, IL: Northwestern University Press, 2011.

Instruktsiia po ispol'zovaniiu perevodchika: http://inojazychniki.livejournal.com/25271.html (Accessed on April 27, 2012)

Jääskeläinen, Riitta. "Are All Professionals Experts? Definitions of Expertise and Reinterpretation of Research Evidence in Process Studies." In *Translation and Cognition*. Ed. Gregory M. Shreve and Erik Angelone. Amsterdam/Philadelphia: John Benjamins Publishing Company, 2010. 213-237.

Jakobson, R. "On Linguistic Aspects of Translation." In *Selected Writings II: Word and Language*. The Hague and Paris: Mouton, [1959] 1971.

Jakobson, R. *Lingvistika i poetika.* "Strukturalizm: 'za' i 'protiv'." Moskva, 1975: www.philology.ru/linguistics/jakobson-75.htm

Jakobson, R. "Linguistics and Poetics." In Pomorska, K. and Rudy, S. (eds.). *Language and Literature*. Cambridge, MA: Belknap Press of Harvard University Press, [1960/9?] 1987.

Kalashnikova, Elena. *Po-russki s liubov'iu: Besedy s perevodchikami. [In Russian with Love: Conversations with translators.*] Moskva: Novoe Literaturnoe Obozrenie, 2008.

Kalashnikova, Elena. Vstrecha s perevodchikom Viktorom Golyshevym. May 12, 2010: http://www.youtube.com/watch?v=ETqLKJF1PNM (Accesssed on May 14, 2012)

Koren, Leonard. *Which 'Aesthetics' Do You Mean? Ten Definitions*. Point Reyes, CA: Imperfect Publishing, 2010.

Lanchikov, V. K. "Istoricheskaia stilizatsiia v sinkhronicheskom khudozhestvennom perevode."["Historical Stylization in Synchronic Literary Translation."] Perevod i diskurs. Vestnik MGLU. Moskva: MGLU, No. 463 (2002): 115-122

Lanchikov, V.K. and Meshalkina, Ye.N. "Kitaitsy na mskarade, ili Khudlo ot Nastika." ["Chinese Guys at a Masked Ball, or 'Ficprose' from Nastik."] *Mosty. Zhurnal perevodchikov.* Moskva: R.Valent, No. 3/19 (2008): 12-23.

Lanchikov, V. K. "Razvitie khudozhestvennogo perevoda v Rossii kak evoliutsiia funktsional'noi ustanovki." ["The Development of Literary Translation in Russia as Evolution of Functional Orientations."] *Vestnik of Nizhny Novgorod Linguistics University*. Nizhny Novgorod, Russia: Nizhny Novgorod Linguistics University. Issue No. 4, 2009, pp. 163-172. (This article can also be accessed on the "Thinkaloud" site: http://www.thinkaloud.ru/sciencelr.html.)

Lanchikov, V. K. "Perevod 'tam i togda.' Ob odnoi perevodcheskoi mistifikatsii." ["Translation 'There and Then': The Case of One Translatorial Mystification."] *Mosty. Zhurnal perevodchikov*. Moskva: R.Valent, No. 1/29 (2011): 42.

Lanchikov, V. K. "Topografiia poiska. Standartizatsiia v iazyke hudozhestvennykh perevodov i eë preodolenie." [The Topography of Searching. Standardization in the Language of Fiction Prose Translation and Ways of Overcoming it."] *Mosty. Zhurnal perevodchikov*. Moskva: R.Valent, No. 2/30 (2011): 30-38. (For the second part of this article, see http://www.thinkaloud.ru/feature/lan-topo.pdf.)

Lecercle, Jean-Jacques. *The Violence of Language*. London and New York: Routledge, 1990.

Lecercle, Jean-Jacques. *Interpretation as Pragmatics. Language, Discourse, Society*. New York, N.Y.: St. Martin's Press, Scholarly Division, 1999.

Leighton, Lauren G. (Translator and editor). *The Art of Translation: Kornei Chukovsky's High Art*. Knoxville: University of Tennessee Press, 1984.

Leighton, Lauren G. *Two Worlds, One Art. Literary Translation in Russia and America*. Dekalb: Northern Illinois University Press, 1991.

Lermontov, M. Iu. *Geroi nashego vremeni*. 1840: http://www.klassika.ru/read.html?proza/lermontov/geroi.txt

Lermontov, M. *A Hero of Our Time*. Translated by Natasha Randall. London: Penguin Books Ltd., 2009.

Lermontov, M. Iu. *A Hero of Our Time*. Translated by Marian Schwartz. New York and Toronto: Modern Library Paperback Edition, 2004.

Lermontov, M. Iu. *A Hero of Our Time*. Translated by Paul Foote. London: Penguin Books Ltd., 2001.

Lermontov, M. Iu. *A Hero of Our Time*. Translated by Vladimir Nabokov and Dmitri Nabokov (1958). Boston, Massachusetts: Overlook TP, 2009.

May, Rachel. *The Translator in the Text. On Reading Russian Literature in English*. Evanston, IL: Northwestern University Press, 1994.

Merton, Robert K. *Qualitative and Quantitative Social Research: Papers in Honor of Paul Lazarsfeld*. New York: Free Press, 1979.

Merton, Robert K. *Theory and Social Structure*. New York, N.Y.: The Free Press, 1964.

Merton, Robert K. *Social Theory and Social Structure*. Revised and enlarged edition. London: The Free Press of Glencoe, 1957.

Miles, M.B. and Huberman, A.M. *Qualitative Data Analysis*. Second edition. Thousand Oaks, CA: SAGE Publications, 1994.

Norton, David. *The King James Bible: A Short History from Tyndale to Today*. Cambridge: Cambridge University Press, 2011.

Ortega y Gasset, José. *The Revolt of the Masses*. [*La Rebelión de Las Masas* (1930).] New York, N. Y: W. W. Norton & Company, Inc., 1994.

Parks, Tim. *Translating Style: A Literary Approach to Translation – A Translation Approach to Literature*. Second Edition. Manchester, UK & Kinderhook, N. Y., USA: St. Jerome Publishing, 2007.

Parks, Tim. "Mysteries of the Meta-Task." In *The Iowa Review Forum on Literary Translation*. Retrieved on November 21, 2011 from: http://iowareview.uiowa.edu/?q=page/mysteries_of_the_metatask

Penrose, Roger. *Shadows of the Mind: A Search for the Missing Science of Consciousness*. Oxford: Oxford University Press, 1996.

Platonov, Andrey. *The Foundation Pit*. Translated from the Russian by Robert Chandler and Geoffrey Smith. London: The Harvill Press, 1996.

Platonov, Andrey. *Kotlovan. Tekst, materialy tvorcheskoi istorii*. Sankt-Peterburg: Nauka, 2000.

Platonov, Andrey. *The Foundation Pit*. A new translation from the definitive Russian text by Robert & Elizabeth Chandler and Olga Meerson. With notes and an afterword by Robert Chandler and Olga Meerson. New York, NY: New York Review Books, 2009.

Postrel, Steven R. and Feser, Edward. "Reality Principles: An Interview with John R. Searle." *Reason Magazine*. February 2000 issue. 1-6. Retrieved on July 20, 2010 from: http://reason.com/archives/2000/02/01/reality-principles-an-intervie

Punch, Keith F. *Introduction to Social Research. Quantitative and Qualitative Approaches*. London, Thousand Oaks, CA, New Delhi: SAGE Publications, 1998.

Salindzher, Dzh. D. *Sobranie sochinenii. Lovets na khlebnom pole*. Perevod s angliiskogo Maksima Nemtsova. Moskva: Eksmo, 2008.

Salindzher, Dzherom D. *Nad propast'iu vo rzhi*. Perevod s angliiskogo Rity Rait-Kovalevoi. Moskva: Eksmo, 2010a.

Salindzher, Dzherom David. *Nad propast'iu vo rzhi*. Perevod s angliiskogo Iakova Lotovskogo. Zhurnal *Sem' iskusstv*, No. 2 (2010b): http://7iskusstv.com/2010/Nomer2/Lotovsky1.php (last accessed February 8, 2014).

Salinger, J.D. *The Catcher in the Rye*. New York, Boston, London: Little, Brown and Company, 1991.

Schopenhauer, Arthur. *Essays and Aphorisms*. Selected and Translated with an Introduction by R.J. Hollingdale. London: Penguin Books, 1970.

Searle, John R. *Speech Acts*. Cambridge: Cambridge University Press, 1969.

Searle, John R. *Intentionality*. Cambridge: Cambridge University Press, 1983 (a).

Searle, John R. "The Word Turned Upside Down." *The New York Review of Books*. October 27, 1983 (b): http://www.nybooks.com/articles/archives/1983/oct/27/the-word-turned-upside-down/.

Searle, John R. "An Exchange on Deconstruction" (Reply to Louis H. Mackey). *The New York Review of Books*, February 2, 1984: http://www.nybooks.com/articles/archives/1984/feb/02/an-exchange-on-deconstruction/?page=3.

Searle, John R. "Rationality and Realism: What is at stake?" *Daedalus*, Fall 1993.

Searle, John R. *Mind, Language, and Society: Philosophy in the Real World*. New York: Basic Books, 1998.

Searle, John R. *Rationality in Action*. Cambridge, Mass.: MIT Press, 2001.

Searle John R. "Toward a Unified Theory of Reality." *Harvard Review of Philosophy*, No. 12 (2004): 93-135.

Searle, John R. *Mind: A Brief Introduction (Foundations of Philosophy)*. Oxford: Oxford University Press, 2005.

Searle, John R. *Philosophy in a New Century: Selected Essays*. Cambridge: Cambridge University Press, 2008.

Searle, John R. "Why Should You Believe It?" *The New York Review of Books*. September 24, 2009: 88-92.

Searle, John R. *Making the Social World: The Structure of Human Civilization*. Oxford/New York: Oxford University press, 2010.

Sergay, Timothy. "New but Hardly Improved: Are Multiple Retranslations of Classics the Best Cultural Use to Make of Translation Talent?" *Russian Language Journal* (RLJ). Volume 61 (2011): 33-50.

Shreve, Gregory. "Knowing Translation: Cognitive and Experiential Aspects of Translation Expertise from the Perspective of Expertise Studies." In *Translation Studies: Perspectives on an Emerging Discipline*. Alessandra Riccardi (ed.). Cambridge: Cambridge University Press, 2002. 150-171.

Shreve, Gregory. "The Deliberate Practice: Translation and Expertise." In *Journal of Translation Studies*, No. 9/1 (2006): 27-42.

Shreve, Gregory. "Recipient Orientation and Metacognition in the Translation Process." In *Minding the Translation Receiver*. Rodica Dimitriu (editor). Brussels: Les Edition du Hazard, 2009.

Shreve, Gregory M. and Angelone, Erik (editors). *Translation and Cognition*. Amsterdam and Philadelphia: John Benjamins Publishing Company, 2010.

Shreve, Gregory M and Angelone Erik. "Translation and Cognition. Recent Developments." In *Translation and Cognition*. Ed. Gregory M. Shreve and Erik Angelone. Amsterdam/Philadelphia: John Benjamins Publishing Company, 2010. 1-13.

Steiner, George. *After Babel. Aspects of Language and Translation*. Third edition. Oxford, New York: Oxford University Press, 1998.

Stephens, Mitchell. "Jacques Derrida and Deconstruction." *The New York Times Magazine*. January 23, 1994. Retrieved on July 19, 2010 from: http://www.nyu.edu/classes/stephens/Jacques%20Derrida%20-%20NYT%20-%20page.htm.

Venuti, Lawrence, ed. *The Translator's Invisibility: A History of Translation*. London/New York: Routledge, 1995.

Venuti, Lawrence. *The Scandals of Translation*. London/New York: Routledge, 1998.

Venuti, Lawrence, ed. *The Translation Studies Reader*. London and New York: Routledge, 2000.

Venuti, Lawrence. "Towards a Translation Culture." In *The Iowa Review Forum on Literary Translation*. Retrieved on November 21, 2011 from: http://iowareview.uiowa.edu/page/towards_a_translation_culture

Wood, James. "In a Spa Town." (*A Hero of Our Time* by Mikhail Lermontov, translated by Natasha Randall.) *The New York Review of Books*. Vol. 32, No. 3, 11 February 2010: 19-21.

Wood, James. Interview on the *Marketplace of Ideas* (A public radio show about books, commerce, culture and fascinating concepts) on September 16, 2008: http://colinmarshall.libsyn.com/index.php?post_id=380948

Wood, James. *How Fiction Works*. New York: Farrar, Straus and Giroux, 2008.

9 783659 519857